# PASSIONATE PATRON:

## THE LIFE OF ALEXANDER HARDCASTLE

### AND THE GREEK TEMPLES OF AGRIGENTO

ALEXANDRA RICHARDSON

© Alexandra Richardson and Archaeopress 2009

Archaeopress
Gordon House
276 Banbury Road
Oxford
OX2 7ED

www.archaeopress.com

ISBN 978 1 905739 28 8

All rights reserved. No part of this book may be reproduced, stored in retrieval system, or transmitted, in any form or by any means, electronic, mechanical, photocopying or otherwise, without the prior written permission of the copyright owners.

Printed and bound in Great Britain by
Marston Book Services Ltd, Oxfordshire

Cover illustrations

Alexander Hardcastle, *c.* 1922
The Temple of Heracles, Agrigento (photo: the author)

# CONTENTS

| | |
|---|---|
| Acknowledgements | i |
| Introduction | v |
| Chapter 1 | 1 |
| Chapter 2 | 5 |
| Chapter 3 | 13 |
| Chapter 4 | 19 |
| Chapter 5 | 26 |
| Chapter 6 | 34 |
| Chapter 7 | 42 |
| Chapter 8 | 47 |
| Chapter 9 | 52 |
| Chapter 10 | 59 |
| Chapter 11 | 64 |
| Chapter 12 | 72 |
| Chapter 13 | 79 |
| Chapter 14 | 83 |
| Chapter 15 | 85 |
| Chapter 16 | 92 |
| Chapter 17 | 95 |
| Chapter 18 | 99 |
| Chapter 19 | 103 |
| Chapter 20 | 105 |
| Chapter 21 | 109 |
| Chapter 22 | 112 |
| Chapter 23 | 116 |
| Chapter 24 | 120 |
| Epilogue | 125 |
| Sources | 135 |
| About the Author | 143 |

# ACKNOWLEDGEMENTS

I would like to acknowledge the many individuals who patiently and generously gave me their time and their expertise over the four years it took to bring this book to fruition. I only regret that, together with those listed in alphabetical order below, there are many, many others – valued archivists, town historians and librarians – who remain nameless but who nonetheless were vital to my work.

My grateful thanks go to: Salvatore Alaimo the retired custodian who took me around Alexander Hardcastle's Villa Aurea on several occasions, opening out-of-bounds doors to the Englishman's favourite terrace; Dr Giovanni Amodeo of Agrigento's Psychiatric Hospital who patiently found information from the hospital archives on Hardcastle's condition and answered questions about his case; Prof. Marcello Barbanera of Rome's La Sapienza University who shed light on techniques of the times for resurrecting Greek columns; Prof. Settimio Biondi who provided some of the early leads into Hardcastle's ancestry; Mrs Rita Boswell of the Harrow School Archives who dug out details of young Alexander's academic achievements along with rare early photographs of him and his older brother Joseph; Francesco Consolo who briefed me on bits of Agrigento history that I would not otherwise have known; Prof. Valeria D'Atri of the Soprintendenza all'Archeologia per l'Etruria Meridionale in Rome who generously gave me full access to the papers relating to Hardcastle's work in the Viterbo and Ferento areas; Dr A.E.L. Davis who wrote the entry on Frances Hardcastle for The Oxford Dictionary of National Biography and supplied me with a copy of the all-important will of Alexander's father; Gabriele De Angelis who shared memories of his father Cesare who first urged Hardcastle to come to Agrigento; Michele Di Dio of Sicily's Archivio Fotografico Regionale; Jacsin Finger of the Maria Mitchell Association on Nantucket who uncovered accounts of the renown American astronomer and her memorable encounter with the Herschel clan; Mimmo Franzinelli who authored several books on the fascist period in Italy; Dott.a Lucina Gandolfo and her formidable team at the A. Salinas Regional Archaeological Museum in Palermo who gave me free run of the field reports on and photography of digs throughout the 1920s and 1930s in Agrigento; Beatrice Gozzo who checked the Whitaker family correspondence at the Villa Malfitano in Palermo; Carey Graziano church warden of the Holy Cross Anglican Church in Palermo who pulled out cumbersome volumes on the history of her church where Henry Robert Hardcastle occasionally preached; Mr E.J.B. Hardcastle of Wadhurst in East Sussex who filled me in on some of the prolific family tree in England; Simonetta Agnello Hornby who at the very outset gave me the all-important push to start this adventure in her homeland; Gerardo Kaiser of the British Consulate in Naples who gave me on extended loan his personal copy of the only little booklet on Hardcastle's work in Sicily; Ambassador Guido Lenzi the diplomatic advisor to the Minister of the Interior in Rome who, together with Ambassador Leonardo Visconti chief of Diplomatic Protocol at the Ministry of Foreign Affairs helped clear up points about the honour bestowed on Hardcastle by the Italian Government; Prof. Pio Luigi Lo Bue who ever-willingly helped me with local history in Agrigento; Prof. Clemente Marconi, the J.R. McCredie Professor of Greek Art and Archaeology at the Institute of Fine Arts in New York who overwhelmed me with a cache of xeroxed correspondence between Hardcastle and his own great-uncle the archaeologist Pirro Marconi; Dott.a Marina Marconi – Pirro's daughter - who received me in Palermo to talk about her father; Calogero Miceli who is perhaps the last person alive in Agrigento to remember his childhood meetings with Hardcastle and who showed me the still flourishing tree that the Englishman gave to his family; Simon Moody at the National Army Museum in London who kindly read my military section and recommended improvements; John Pemble in Bristol who put together a formidable reading list to start me off; Prof. Patrizio Pensabene of La Sapienza University in Rome who explained a lot about Hardcastle's work at Ferento; John and Jonathan Prag who respectively got me into the Warburg Institute Library where I first began my archaeological research and painstakingly read my manuscript with an expert eye; David Ridgway in London who, early on, gave me more valuable tips and contacts than I could count; Dott.a Isabella Scichilone of Aragona, Sicily who generously let me consult her university thesis on Hardcastle; Valerie Scott, Librarian at the British School at Rome who set me right on the history of the School and the many books in her domain; Dr Riccardo Serafini in Milan who patiently interpreted the course of Hardcastle's mental sickness; Dr Gillian Shepherd lecturer in Classical Archaeology at the University of Birmingham who read my manuscript and made many valuable suggestions; John Herschel-Shorland who gave me access to the Herschel archives he so meticulously keeps and made suggestions on the Herschel part of my manuscript; Avv. Francesco Sinatra in Agrigento who was the very first person in Sicily to lend a helping hand and introduce me to all the key players there and later was to supply me with the largest photocopies I have ever seen; Raleigh Trevelyan who kindly went through all his Whitaker files to hunt for Alexander; Arch. Gaetano Tripodi of the Soprintendenza Beni Culturali ed Ambientali di Agrigento who piloted my access into his office for an all-too-short study of the original Hardcastle correspondence on file there; Dr Alexandra Villing curator in the British Museum's Department of Greek and Roman Antiquities who let me study the plaster copies of relics which Hardcastle sent to London from Agrigento; Emily Winterburn formerly curator of Astronomy at the Royal Observatory, Greenwich who read and made suggestions on the Herschel chapters.

The people who, *per forza*, defy alphabeticising here are three in number. All of them are precious to me for the unfailing help and encouragement they gave me unstintingly over four years, never showing a moment of impatience. In Ireland, Debonnaire Hardcastle Perceval, who is Alexander's great-niece, and her husband Sandy opened their door and their hearts to me and let me ransack trunks and trunks of family papers, journals and photograph albums in their attic for days on end ('whatever it takes'), urging me along with hot tea and mushroom soup. Piecing together the life of her elusive relative would have been impossible without her help. In Agrigento, Ermogene La Foreste, a veteran reporter for Sicily's L'Ora newspaper and head of the Fondazione Alexander Hardcastle believed in the project from Day One. No question, no material, no favour was ever too big or too difficult for him. He shared his wealth of knowledge generously throughout and allowed me to understand Sicily much better. I am deeply grateful for his friendship. Last but certainly not least, there is Tom. My steadying Rock of Gibraltar. Thank you.

# INTRODUCTION

My very first encounter with Alexander Hardcastle was hardly the most promising. It was on the proverbial dusky winter evening, racing up the curving Sicilian road to Agrigento. My husband and I were running late for an appointment. The lights on the Valley of the Temples' breathtaking Greek monuments had just been switched on, bathing the sweeping columns in a golden hue. Someone in the car then pointed out the unilluminated outline of a villa: *'Ecco la casa dell'inglese!'* Then and there, I did not make the connection between the temples and the *inglese*. We hurried on. Later that evening, a small booklet was thrust into my hands. It had a light blue cover and was entitled 'Alexander Hardcastle: l'uomo, l'archeologo, il suo tempo'. I tucked it first into my suitcase and, then later, onto a back shelf of our library.

I never truly forgot about the book, yet, strangely, never got around to reading it either. Another few years went by; after transferring back to London and temporarily borrowing someone else's copy, I at last retrieved my own and began reading. In essence, it was a compilation of talks delivered at a 1984 symposium devoted entirely to the Englishman's life and achievements. What emerged was an account of a remarkable man who wholly dedicated his later life and finances to restoring and excavating what is surely one of the finest classical Greek sites in the Western Mediterranean. I rapidly began to be drawn in to the sketchy, sometimes speculative, details surrounding the remarkable Captain Hardcastle. I knew then that I had to 'do something about it'.

I thought back to his unlit villa beside the theatrically shining temples, and the more I got to know the man, the more it seemed entirely in keeping with his personality that his former home should *still* not be sharing the spotlight with the great monuments he was so intimately involved with. He remained a mysterious and private person who kept his own counsel throughout life. I was to discover that he wrote very few letters home to his family from the Far East, South Africa, Italy. And when he *did* write to the chosen few, I had to learn to read between the lines. Luckily his own family wrote to one another making mention of him. A vital building block for me. With so little to go on, it was just the sort of challenge that a researcher relishes. The Anglo-Italian theme was yet another appeal, my instinctive habitat. No full-scale biography had ever been written about him and thus I was not stepping on any toes. I had the field all to myself, piecing together a profile from many sources, set largely in a period of modern Sicilian history, the 1920s and early '30s rarely 'popularised' by foreign writers. That was all how the journey began.

*****

Research would initially take me to Sicily, and later, to Ireland and many places in England. In Agrigento, like a pebble in a stream, I was swept along from one site to another, making new contacts. Some of them became good and loyal friends, none more so than Ermogene La Foreste of the Alexander Hardcastle Foundation. I would return many times to the island, adding to the mosaic of information. That was the 'easy' part.

Back in England, the immediate challenge was to track down one of Alexander Hardcastle's closest descendents – a great-niece – whose first name I had been given in Agrigento. I suspected that she would be 'camouflaged' by her married name, an added difficulty. I turned, as one does these days, to the internet. After many serendipitous tries, the trail got warmer. The very first break was a first-person account by a man in Ireland who had been suffering severe allergic reactions to certain pesticides and other noxious fumes. Buried in his text was a full-name reference to his wife. Her first name tallied exactly with the one I had been given in Sicily, save one minor misspelling. There, too, was her maiden name, Hardcastle! It would lead me to her home in Ireland. Things fell into place after that and, slowly, I was able to take the tale forward.

Sorting out names went further than that, however. When I telephoned her the very first time to tell her about my biography project, she exclaimed, 'Oh, Alick!' It was early days still and I had, as yet, not heard him called by that name. When we met in Ireland and I began sifting through the cornucopia of family papers, my confusion grew: all of his relatives had seemingly adopted their own preferred spellings of his nickname. To some, he was 'Alec'. To others, he was 'Alic' or 'Alick'. Hardcastle himself did not always make things easy: he often signed off simply as 'AH'. Just enough papers survive, however, where he styles himself as 'Alick' for me to have settled on this last version. His own.

But the word labyrinth does not end there. Today's 'Agrigento' has also undergone bewildering changes of name over time. I elaborate what they were and when they changed. Thereafter, I use the appropriate name for the period discussed. Adding to the complications is the fact that in its earliest incarnation, the Greek settlement was called Akragas but was sometimes popularly transliterated as Acragas in English. I have opted for the former version. Lastly, in *most* cases I give the Agrigento temples their supposed original Greek names rather than the later Roman ones, except in instances where I quote a passage directly from an author's book or where they are more familiarly known in the Roman version.

*Buona lettura.*

*'Ma da un altro venne la possibilità di questo lavoro, ed esso è il gentiluomo inglese Commendatore Alexander Hardcastle, straniero di nascita ma agrigentino di elezione, mecenate di ricerche archeologiche e di tante opere utili agli uomini. Dalla sua generosità hanno avuto alimento le campagne di scavi da vari anni condotte sul suolo agrigentino, che tanta messe di novità hanno dato e tanta luce hanno fatto sull'illustre città siceliota, ed hanno permesso a me di lavorare di nuovo, di rivelare cose nuove e belle, la fortuna più alta che uno studioso di antichità possa desiderarsi. Appassionato ed instancabile ricercatore, Egli mi ha fornito notizie e tracce preziose; da questa sua personale partecipazione ho tratto frutto, e di sue indicazioni ed idee riconosco di essermi servito, per rendere quanto più possibile completa l'immagine dell'antica città.'*

*Pirro Marconi*

**Agrigento, topografia ed arte 1929**

# -1-

He may not have known it, but he was on his way home, his brother at his side, to a place he had never set eyes on. Disembarking from the overnight steamer from the mainland at the Molo Santa Lucia, the two men made their way across Palermo to the grandly arcaded railroad station and boarded their carriage for the onward leg of the journey.

When they at last stepped down from their train and stretched their stiffened limbs, they were numbed by the five-hour, 84-mile journey through the stark heartland of Sicily. Their train had chugged along the northern coastline out of Palermo as far as Cerda, taking in vistas out to sea of the colourful little blue, yellow and red fishing boats with their sails fluttering in the chop. The tracks had then veered inland to Roccapalumba where the terrain abruptly turns sterile and stony and where they had alighted for the onward connection south, continuing past the vultured vestiges of Norman castles, on down towards the coast. Meagre riverbeds, first the Torto, later the Platani, made half-hearted appearances alongside the tracks, offering not much allure to the onboard passengers other than the view of occasional clumps of greenery hinting at the impending arrival of spring.

Like the landscape, the island itself had rarely known abundance or serenity over the centuries. That pattern remained unchanged. Its estates were mostly in the tight grip of the aristocracy and there was scant sign that that grip would loosen any time soon to bring economic advantage to the underclass. Indeed, maintaining the status quo seemed high on the agenda of the wealthy, the better for keeping downtrodden peasants firmly under control on this thankless land. By the outset of World War I, dogged by endemic disease, hunger and illiteracy, one and a half million islanders finally had put down their humble work tools and left. The vacuum that they left behind drove home to the central government and the world at large the message of just how wide a gap there had been between rich and poor and how very little Rome cared or responded to reports on the conditions there. Emigrant remittances, to be sure, brought a welcomed injection of cash to those who stayed behind, an injection that amounted to as much as 100 million Lire a year. The sores nonetheless remained, open and festering. The two men, had they looked hard enough from their train window, might have seen first snatches of what they would later come to know first hand a lot better: miles of Spartan, broken-down hovels dotting the scenery, water jug-bearing donkeys providing basic drink to the thirsty, scrofulous children alive with pus-oozing sores, strips of rags that passed as clothing adorning the backs of many, and further south, a thick haze of sulphur – the island's so-called 'yellow gold' – emanating from over one hundred mines. A haze that hovered scarcely off the ground, discharging an acrid smell into the air. Had it borne a distinct sound all of its own, the two men might, too, have discerned the first faint distant rumblings of a political system that would in coming years make itself all too nastily heard throughout Italy: that of fascism.

At last at their destination, they elbowed their way past the small thicket of railroad porters pleading for their custom and exited the long, two-storied station set deep in a dip between the hills and flanked by a handful of lonely farmhouses. Several carriages stood nearby, their horses listlessly whisking flies from their flanks. They were waiting to transport arriving passengers up the steep and dusty track to the town high above. Stuffing their no-longer-needed rail tickets into their pockets, they studied the conveyances on offer. Would these two *nglisi* – foreigners – favour *cocchiere* Pignocco, Quartararo or Bennici with their custom and luggage? It little mattered as they stood momentarily transfixed and wordless by the scene before them. The spell quickly broken, they clambered aboard one and began their slow ascent to town. The true magnet of the place – one of the prime Greek classical sites of southern Italy – lay out of view, on the southern side of the plateau.

It was an age when archaeology, whether in Sicily, mainland Italy, Greece, Egypt or elsewhere, stirred public imagination. Sir Arthur John Evans, a handsome Englishman in his late forties, had uncovered the Palace of Minos at Knossos in Crete, the treasures of which had dazzled London viewers in a first showing in 1903. In Egypt, Howard Carter, at 48, had just found the stairway into the royal tomb of Tutankhamun on November 4, 1922. Exciting discoveries were being made elsewhere too, sometimes even by rank amateurs. And their findings all were broadcast boldly across the pages of the major newspapers and magazines back home, captivating rapt readers. The reports seemed almost a beckoning, an open invitation to pack one's shovel and head off. The magnificent remains that lay just beyond the sight of the two men had lured many throughout the ages, including one of their own very famous ancestors. Pindar had seen them. Goethe, too. And Lord Byron. William Gladstone had arrived on muleback. Alexandre Dumas, Guy de Maupassant, Brahms all made the trek, while the Prince of Siam trained it more comfortably in from Taormina.[1] For the time being, however, it remained a treat later in store for the two Englishmen.

Cached between the rocky folds of the plateau that they were now hugging in their carriage was a honeycomb of caves. Damp and dark and utterly barren, these were home to herds of sheep and sometimes even to the most wretched of the town's indigent, those who could not even afford modest palm frond-roofed huts as shelter. No doubt the two travellers, like all others, were silently studied as their carriage strained to pull its human cargo ever upwards, past these ragged, barefooted denizens in their lightless refuges. Up on top, in neatly stratified geography lay moneyed life of a far wealthier order, of the

---

[1] One who did *not* succumb to the spell was Victorian lepidopterist Margaret Fountaine who, when she reached Girgenti in 1896 sniffed 'the ruined temples are very famous, but I do not care for antiquities'. Butterflies were her bent above almost all else.

## Chapter 1

propertied classes. A few heavy-lidded aristocrats interrupted their *conversazioni* and ambled over from the comfort of plush sofas to peer out the sun-bleached curtains of their social-club windows: what visitors had that day's train disgorged into their midst? From the Via Imera, the carriage slowly entered the sombre, lava-paved main Piazza Vittorio Emanuele, passed near the large Prefecture, then turned sharply left by the *carabinieri* police station and into the steep incline towards the Via San Vito. Pulling up at the front entrance to Number 30, the Hotel Belvedere, the coachman announced 'we are here' as he hopped down to offload their suitcases. Scarcely twelve months had gone by since the Belvedere had changed premises.

It was neither the town's very best hotel, nor its worst. But, respectable, in 1905 it had hosted the likes of Dom Pedro d'Alcantara, grandson of the last Emperor of Brazil, as well as a Nobel Prize laureate in literature, historian Theodor Mommsen. In Via San Vito, the new purpose-built Belvedere featured far more modest terraces with south-facing vistas of farmhouse roofs and of the sea beyond. Alas, there were no longer the two white tiled terraces and vast pots of red carnations that had been so striking at the earlier location. It had also shed 'the ludicrous mixture of ancient splendour and modern trash, immense sofas covered in Genoese gold brocade … rickety wardrobes and makeshift washstands … floors covered with old … tiles in yellow and blue …', as one patron so haughtily recorded. On the other hand, the new Belvedere was central and spanking new and several stories high, with accommodation for thirty-five guests. *And* it served bread and butter at the breakfast table, just the way foreigners liked it, in the elegant little dining room so amusingly trimmed with a wrap-around frieze in deep red colour of prancing goats! Goats were the virtual mascots of the town and this was one place where they actually charmed the two Englishmen.

As the two settled their four-Lire fare, the portly young *patron* strode forth from within to welcome his new guests and steer them effusively into the small wood-panelled foyer. The two cast their eyes about, taking in their exotic surroundings: the proprietor had transferred his family collection of painted Sicilian ceramic figurines from the old place, all of them garishly clad in regional costumes. Chunks of minerals, painted vases and rare fans added a further splash to the colourful décor. Photographs and postcards were piled high on the front desk for souvenir-hungry travellers. Sunk into armchairs here and there were guests, chin on chest, taking a gentle snooze or riffling absent-mindedly through newspapers, perhaps studying the day's offerings off at that new-fangled cinema, the Edison or at the Regina Margherita Theatre where operettas and variety shows were the entertainment *du jour*.

It was mid-winter, 1921, when as one writer, Douglas Sladen, put it tersely, 'Sicily has the prime claim on the English traveller … it is near its best when England is at its worst.' England was still emerging from the tragic aftermath of a world war that had taken its dreadful toll of 723,000 dead. The government was still exhorting its citizens to 'Eat Slowly: You will need less food'. The Spanish flu pandemic of 1918-1919, as well, had left England with 250,000 of its sons perished. And albeit on a far less catastrophic level, the weather, particularly in the winter, was nothing to stick around for, particularly if you *could* travel south, where the mean annual temperature of Sicily stood at 64.2°F. On all counts, then, it had been time to leave. The two Englishmen were Alexander Hardcastle and his younger brother, Henry Robert Hardcastle and they had just left far behind the grand trappings of their wellborn family to travel to Girgenti on the southern coast of Sicily. Trappings that had included sound investments, fine mansions, clipped lawns, uniformed servants, a heady social circle and a plethora of parasoled aunts. The necessaries for their new surroundings there in Girgenti, suggested one observer, would henceforth be *'a walking stick and a contemplative mind'*. Alexander and his brother had, providentially, come fully equipped with both. Ahead lay a bold new chapter of Alexander's life, the one for which he would forever be remembered in his new and still unfamiliar surroundings.

# −2−

The stirrings of the long journey south to Sicily had begun many years and several generations earlier, amidst the thick tangle of a prolific and gene-gifted family. This was an urbane clan, part of which was foreign. They travelled. They befriended and corresponded with many of the great thinkers both in England and abroad. Some worked in distant lands. Most of them spoke several languages comfortably. They moved about easily and without fuss.

Alexander's mother Maria Sophia was the daughter of Sir John Frederick Herschel and his wife Margaret Brodie Stewart. Maria Sophia was the granddaughter of Sir William Herschel, who started out his illustrious life in England as a penniless émigré from Hanover, Germany. Both father and grandfather were primarily noted for their distinguished work as astronomers. But as inveterate polymaths, the two were earnestly absorbed in other high-minded pursuits as well. Indeed, her grandfather William was a gifted oboist and organist in his young adulthood.

On his arrival in England in the late 1750s, he drifted from job to job in – among other places – Richmond (Yorkshire), Newcastle, Leeds, Halifax and finally, in early 1767, Bath. There, William was appointed organist at the Octagon Chapel. He composed his own music and directed the Bath public concerts. But his interests started tugging him towards astronomy. The more he gazed through the lens of a telescope, the more he wanted to extend the view. Hiring stronger telescopes, or indeed buying them outright, was out of the question on cost grounds. The time had come to make telescopes himself, in the basement workshop of home. Activity escalated and soon his devoted sister Caroline noted that 'I saw almost every room turned into a workshop'. Caroline Lucretia Herschel, who had recently arrived from Hanover and William's brother Alexander Herschel, who by profession actually was a violoncellist, helped him in this endeavour. When the three siblings settled more or less definitively at a house at 19 New King Street, Caroline mostly helped him with his musical commitments and occasionally shared in his 'sweeps' of the skies, while Alexander helped fine-tune the ever more sophisticated mirrors that were needed. Caroline would involve herself more fully in astronomy later on, at Slough.

When deciding between using a refractor or a reflector, the Herschels opted for the latter. A refractor collects its light via a glass lens while the reflector uses a mirror. Casting truly large glass lenses in those days posed technical problems that the two could not easily overcome. Through dogged trial and error, William and Alexander finally achieved the workable mirror of a reflector telescope that they sought. With that, sky gazing took off in earnest.

On March 13, 1781, William discovered Uranus, almost accidentally. As a round nebulous disc moving slowly among the stars, he first thought the sighted object was a comet. Its mean distance from the sun was 1,783,000,000 miles; when the discovery *was* accepted by the authorities, it formally joined the planetary family as the seventh planet in our solar system. Uranus had been spotted over twenty times before by other observers. But they had always mistaken it for a star, unlike Herschel who initially took it to be a comet. Herschel's find understandably propelled him into the limelight and he was soon summoned by King George III and offered an annual stipend of £200 that helped enable him to leave the orchestra and work full-time at his astronomy. William left Bath in 1782 and after four years at various addresses, settled at Slough in 1786, into a comfortable ivy-clad home called 'Observatory House'.

There, two years later, at age fifty, William momentarily broke off his heavenly sweeps, for a more earthly one: to court and brush into matrimony a wealthy widow named Mary Pitt (née Baldwin) in May 1788. Then he promptly resumed his work and by the next year, 1789, had built out on his lawn a 40-foot telescope provided with a 49-inch reflector of his own casting. (The telescope would remain there for fifty years until 1839 when his son dismantled the disintegrated wooden framework.) It was the largest telescope ever erected at that time. And it was with this telescope that William set about to discover two satellites of the planet Saturn, among other things, and in 1787, another two orbiting Uranus. With the help of his sister Caroline, work continued, too, on his opus, cataloguing the nebulae, star clusters and double stars of the northern hemisphere. Among her many other notable achievements, she was to identify eight comets.

In March 1792, Mary and William had their first and only child, John Frederick William Herschel. From his father, the boy inherited his wide-angle mouth, chiselled jaw and rough-hewn good looks, not to mention the inquisitive mind of his elder. He was a studious and serious youngster, shaped, no doubt, by the accomplishments of his father and by the presence in the Herschel orbit of so many eminent friends and associates. Early schooling at nearby Eton was another matter. Although he was academically bright, his mother Mary constantly fretted for his health and perceived frailty and feared about the rough and tumble of a schoolboy's life. It took one view alone of him coerced into a boxing ring, being pummelled by another student, to withdraw him forthwith. Enrolled thereafter in another school close to Slough and reinforced by private lessons at home, young John blossomed. In due course, aged seventeen, he was ready for university and entered St. John's College, Cambridge where he excelled in pure mathematics. By then, still in his teens, he had taken up poetry, played the piano creditably and had become a skilled draftsman. John was elected a Fellow of the Royal Society. A passion for using camera lucida techniques to help him sketch would follow before long. His father, meanwhile, was beginning to pay the price for *his* unyielding crush of work. According to his granddaughter, Constance Lubbock, at age seventy, in 1808, he suffered a nervous breakdown. It was the beginning of an unhappy occurrence that would unsettlingly revisit the family tree. William's adored sister Caroline noted that it was so serious that she worried whether he'd survive. But pull through he did, lasting until 1822 when he died, aged 84.

Dutifully, John remained on at Observatory House with his widowed mother Mary, following in his father's astronomical footsteps, making sweeps of the northern skies and reviewing his late father's studies. In due course, he shouldered the extra burden of becoming President of the Astronomical Society. Life in that now-hushed household was turning ever more mournfully dark and lonely. So absorbed in his work, to the detriment of most all else, the years seemed to be slipping by and middle age approaching. Little *serious* thought had been devoted by the reticent scholar to affairs of the heart. True, there had been two courtships headed in the direction of matrimony. But they had been acrimoniously shipwrecked. John used the bruising aftermaths of both episodes to take Grand Tours to the Continent to mend his pride. The wounds finally healed and the whole awkward business of marriage got shunted to the back burner of his life.

His long-time friend and travelling companion, James Grahame, feared and fretted about this situation, finally stepping in to engineer a bit of earnest matchmaking. He introduced the solitary, overworked bachelor to a lively Scottish widow and her brood of children. One of the daughters quickly caught John's eye. Margaret Brodie Stewart, scarcely 18, had large darting eyes, a luscious coif of thick dark curls and a gentle smile. There was no doubt about it: she was extremely pretty, extremely bright. What was more, she was utterly undeterred by the nearly two-decade gap in their ages. Early in March 1829, the two were married in London at St. Marylebone Parish Church, where Lord Byron was baptised and where Robert Browning wed Elizabeth Barrett. They set up household there in the same neighbourhood. Margaret came from a long line of straight-backed Scottish Presbyterians and was later described by her own daughter's daughter-in-law Theresa as 'generous, good and resilient in character'. By the end of the first year, Margaret and John welcomed the arrival of their firstborn, Caroline Emilia Mary. The parade of progeny proceeded. Isabella came next, in 1831, the same year John received his knighthood. Their first son, William James, was born in 1833. All this while, he had worked hard producing two catalogues: one a list of over 2000 nebulae and star clusters, the other a six-part record of double stars.

They paused procreatively only briefly in order to pack their bags and sail, in November 1833 aboard the *Mountstuart Elphinstone* for the two-month journey to the Cape of Good Hope in Southern Africa. A lovely Dutch farmhouse called Feldhausen, six miles southeast of Cape Town became home. Sir John oversaw the unpacking of his gigantic telescope and then began his grandiose work: he was going to map the nebulae, star clusters and double stars of the *southern* hemisphere, thus filling out William's work. The project would take four years. By all accounts, the South African years were extremely happy for the Herschel family. Another three children were born at Feldhausen. One was their son Alexander Stewart Herschel, born February 5, 1836. He came into the world at one minute and thirty seconds before midnight. This gave his father just enough time to dash out onto the veranda to see Halley's Comet passing through the sky. 'Good data for the horoscope', he quipped about his new son's timing!

There was a steady trickle of stimulating new friends who came to call. Charles Darwin visited. And then there was a young lady who steamed into town aboard the *SS Cornwall* in early October 1836, freshly arrived from England where she had gone to study. She came to join her father and mother for a lengthy sojourn. Both she and her parents, who themselves had arrived from India, needed the fresh South African air to regain their health. The stopover proved to be a milestone in her life. For not only did she meet her future husband Charles Hay Cameron there, 20 years her senior, but also John Herschel, a man she later would describe as her 'Teacher and High Priest'. It is reckoned that Herschel was the one who first instilled in Julia a budding interest in the infant art of photography. In a letter, she told him 'I remember gratefully that the very first information I ever had of Photography in its Infant Life ... was from you'.

Her great artistry as a Victorian photographic portraitist lay still off on the horizon. But in due course, Julia Margaret Cameron would take four memorable pictures of her friend John Frederick Herschel, back home in England, at Collingwood in 1867. They are iconic images to all photography buffs today. Julia would also give her name to one of the Herschel daughters to whom she became godmother.

The four years flew by and Herschel's monumental project was at last completed. The family sailed back home in 1838. Before long, Margaret was pregnant again, this time with Alexander Hardcastle's mother, Maria Sophia. Margaret's husband, who faithfully kept a diary of his daily doings, penned in an economic entry for October 21, 1839:

> Slough to London 8:32-9:25. Sold stock and bought 4000 Exchange bills. Our 7th child and 4th daughter born at 11 p.m. (Maria).

By the very next day, it was clearly back to business, with a mere one-liner in the diary:

> October 22, 1839 – Full moon.[1]

That said, John and Margaret were devoted parents and John would touchingly record:

> January 26, 1840 – Evening with the little bodies.

And:

> January 29, 1840 – One p.m. Dined with the Children.

Anticipating further births in the family - there would be twelve in all - the Herschels moved on April 3, 1840 to the far larger brick-faced 'Collingwood' at Hawkhurst, Kent,

---

[1] To an astronomer, a full moon was tantamount to being unable to star gaze in an over-brightened sky.

purchased for £10,500. (They did, however, hold on to Observatory House at Slough.) Collingwood was 'very extensive' and had large surrounding grounds graced by tall trees and a large pond. An outlying barn did nicely to house what remained of his father's 40-foot telescope, although by then only the tube survived. Indoors, on one of the entranceway walls they hung a copy of Simeon Borden's 1844 map of the state of Massachusetts. Over the fireplace mantel in the dining room went a portrait of Sir William Herschel, while another of Aunt Caroline was in the drawing room, together with marble busts of William, John and John's eldest daughter, also a Caroline.

The eminent American astronomer Maria Mitchell came to visit from her Nantucket Island home off Cape Cod and was enchanted by the informal and welcoming atmosphere that she found. Her experiences were recounted posthumously in an article published by The Century Illustrated Magazine in which she wrote that: 'the family, including servants, numbered some twenty persons. The household was extensive. The table … seemed over-bountiful.' And the young daughters of the household ('the little planetoids'), she observed, 'dressed simply in the mornings and wore white in the evenings.' No doubt that was a plus point to this unfrivolous Quaker-born New Englander. The two astronomers managed to huddle over the weekend exchanging conversation about less earthly matters. Sir John waxed lyrical about the clear South African skies, likened Saturn's satellite rings to children and pulled out manuscripts of his father and aunt, pointing out 'the interesting parts' to his American houseguest. Lady Herschel confessed to Mitchell how she always chose to travel in second class so as to 'make valuable acquaintances and … learn … something of a class whom she could never meet socially'. Mitchell tartly reflected in return on 'the isolation of rank in England'.

But it was at the dining table and before the hearth where she formed her warmest impressions about the unusually strong bonds of the Herschels as a family: 'I could scarcely believe when I saw Sir John Herschel in his family, guessing conundrums with the children, playing at spelling and telling funny anecdotes that he was the same man of whom one had said to me … [he was] not very good-natured.'

Alexander's mother Maria Sophia apparently was absent during part the visit, off seeing a sick neighbour. Now a comely eighteen-year old, she had had the recent excitement of being presented at court.

Life for this music-passionate family meant frequent soirées before the living room hearth, each member playing his or her preferred instrument in tuneful recital. The girls were often garbed in gauzy, silk-like barége gowns – regardless of the weather outdoors! There were poetry readings and a regular December 31$^{st}$ ritual that brought the entire family together to listen to the peal of church bells ushering in the new year. Education of the children followed the norms of the day for the well-to-do: Maria Sophia and her sisters were taught at home by their parents and governesses; some subjects were parcelled out to outside tutors. Art was an important feature, too, in the curriculum and Alexander's mother excelled at it from an early age. At eleven, she painted an enchanting little watercolour of her own younger sister, Matilda Rose, shown in profile with a thick braid artistically bow-tied to the top of her head.

*Portrait of Matilda Rose Herschel in watercolour by her sister Maria Sophia Herschel, aged 11 (Courtesy of the National Maritime Museum, London, Herschel Collection)*

Maria Sophia's father, all this while, seemed to cram, not just pack, more and more into his fraught schedule. Between 1839 and 1844, he had published over 50 scientific papers. Much of the mapping of the Southern Hemisphere was completed. There was that house move. Four more children had come on to the scene. In short, almost atavistically, Sir John was following in his own father's footsteps. And after 1850, adding to his burdens, he had taken on a job as Master of the Mint, a commitment that he profoundly disliked. It meant spending more time in London than he cared for, quartered in a dour house in Harley Street, far from his beloved family in Kent. His eyesight was failing. He felt he was choking on London's pea soup climate. By 1854, overwhelmed and trying to carry on, using ministrations of laudanum, a morphine derivative, he, too, succumbed to a nervous breakdown. But he did not buckle. The Herschel fibre pulled him through. Nonetheless, his family was growing up and he was growing old.

Alexander Hardcastle's mother blossomed into a rare, dignified beauty. Years later, her daughter-in-law Theresa Clive Bayley, who married Alexander's brother Joseph Alfred II and who kept a detailed 'Life Book', described her thus:

> she was very tall and good looking, very well educated in all directions and had beautiful hair with a natural wave in it … . She did shine as a young woman in London in scientific society and that is where she would have been in her true element. She loved beauty – drew and painted well, spoke French and German well, had a keen, well-trained brain … .

But by then, aged twenty-six, she had attracted the attention of the kindly, mild-mannered Henry Hardcastle, one year younger than she. The two courted and married at the Hawkhurst Church in October 1865. The bride's father who by then was deeply occupied in another interest of his, translating works from the Greek classics, wrote distractedly in his diary:

> October 12, 1865: Finished 23rd book of Iliad. Maria married to H. Hardcastle, son of Joseph Alfred Hardcastle MP for Bury St. Edmunds.

The honeymoon was delayed for over a month. Herschel père recorded hastily:

> November 16th: H. Hardcastle & Maria with Maid left for a tour of Rome.

Henry's sister Mary Josephine remembered her own impressions of the new bride:

> … how much we admired [her] when she first came to us in October 1865. She was an exceedingly graceful elegant woman. I remember our pride and pleasure when she was presented at the Drawing room … I can see her now in a very well made dress of very pale lilac satin with Gloire de Dijon roses and the necklace of 5 rows of pearls which my father … gave her. She was 10 years older than I was. I 16 and she 26 or 27 – too wide a difference for any great intimacy. I think we sympathised most over our love of drawing … . I think their visit to Rome, the winter of 1865-66 were her happiest months and the sketches she did in Rome were very clever.

When Maria Sophia's father died six years later at Collingwood, May 11, 1871, aged 79, John Frederick Herschel's stature was such to warrant burial in the north aisle of Westminster Abbey. At midday May 31, Sir John's plain oak coffin arrived by train from Kent at Charing Cross Station and was borne west solemnly past Trafalgar Square, down Whitehall and into the nave by the cloister entrance of Westminster Abbey. Among the pallbearers was the Duke of Devonshire, Chancellor of Cambridge University; the white-bearded Charles Darwin stood by, amidst the mourners, reflecting, perhaps, back on their happy encounters in South Africa. The Royal Society in London, with which Sir John had had a lifetime's involvement, stated sorrowfully that 'British science has sustained a loss greater than any which it has suffered since the death of [Isaac] Newton, and not one likely to be soon replaced'. Herschel's burial place in the Abbey is marked today by a handsome slab of black Belgian marble with an inscription in Latin. The Dean of Westminster Abbey, Arthur Penrhyn Stanley, delivered the eulogy in fine oratorial prose saying of Sir John: 'It was his peculiar privilege to combine with those more special studies such a width of view, and such a power of expression, as to make him an interpreter, a poet of science, even beyond his immediate sphere.' He added that during early college years 'young Herschel' with two or three of his friends vowed that 'they would put their shoulders to the wheel and leave the world better than they found it'. Alexander was born only 18 months after his famous grandfather's death. No doubt, though, he came to know and be inspired by this illustrious resting spot, and take personally to heart that famous vow.

# -3-

If Alexander's maternal ancestors were largely lodged in the stars, then his father's antecedents were decidedly more earth-anchored. Born in 1815 at Hatcham House, Surrey, Alexander's paternal grandfather Joseph Alfred Hardcastle was the eldest son of Alfred Hardcastle. Educated at Trinity College, Cambridge, Joseph Alfred married young – aged 25 – to Frances Lambirth in 1840. The following year, he was called to the bar at the Inner Temple, but never practised law, opting instead for politics. His stout, round-faced and aquiline-nosed wife Frances, who parted her hair severely down the middle, inherited a comfortable life interest from her grandfather in a flourishing brewery in the idyllic green-lawned Essex village of Writtle, just to the west of Chelmsford. It was an interest that would help cushion the costs of her husband's ambitions in public office, first as Liberal MP for Colchester (1847-1852), then for Bury St. Edmunds (1857-1874).

'Home' was mostly on his wife's territory at Writtle and it was on the grand scale. Their five children – one son and four daughters – were brought up in a setting where home was simply called 'The Rectory' and villagers needed no further explanations as to which building that might mean. Henry, Alexander's father, was the firstborn into this graceful, well-oiled world in December 1840 at The Rectory. It was a home on which his father over the years lavished the not inconsiderable sum of £20,000, or today's £13.2 million. In accounts that he wrote as an adult, Henry reminisced about how he had been a victim of bullying at Harrow School. Early photographs of him show that he was not the barrel-chested braggart sort to punch back at his adversaries. Like his own Papa, after an idyllic childhood in this manicured setting where the only hum on the horizon for awhile was that of the brewery spewing out the wherewithal to keep up this unsullied lifestyle, Henry took the path to Trinity College, Cambridge, just like countless others of his relatives, past and future. His sister Frances Alice was born four years after Henry. She grew up and married locally, to Thomas Usborne, there in Writtle. Her husband was described as a man 'who inherited money, made money and married money'. They settled into 'The House'. The 3-story brick mansion she henceforth called home was crowned by 7 chimneys. It was surrounded by trim lawns, greenhouses, quarters for numerous carriages, stabling for 24 horses. It was a celebration and a statement of position. The Hardcastles and their spouses, in short, were Someone.

There was a staff of thirteen servants and a further battery of grooms and gardeners to look after the outdoor work. She and Thomas filled that grand ménage with six daughters and six sons. Next in the filial procession after the births of Henry and Frances

Alice came Emma Winifred, followed by Mary Josephine in 1847. Mary Josephine attended the Slade School of Art and went on to marry Robert Collier, later the Baron Monkswell. She distinguished herself in adult life with well-written diaries about social and political life in London. They were published posthumously in two volumes to great acclaim. In 'A Victorian Diarist: Extracts from the Journals of Mary, Lady Monkswell 1873-1895' and '1895-1909', Mary Josephine gave a lively, unbridled account of everyone and everything that she saw and did in those years. The last of the Hardcastle children to be born was Emily Eliza who grew up and settled in Scotland with her husband. Unlike his father, young Henry stuck with his law studies, becoming a barrister of the Inner Temple. But as a career, it seemingly had a short shelf life. He dabbled in writing legal tracts for publication with such dry titles as 'The Law and Practice of Election Petitions'. And so it is no surprise that on the Writtle register of Baptisms recording the births of his own first two children Henry was initially recorded as 'barrister' in 1866. But, the very next year, with the birth of the second child, he was entered *tout court* as 'esquire'. Parental handouts of some £1200 per year, about £600,000 in today's money, did not make toil a necessity. Besides, he had taken on the management of the brewery.

As time went on, though, his father's affairs turned murky, and hidden facts began to leak out. His political ambitions, quite simply, were beyond his purse. Overspending, rewriting the accounts, bribes paid to smooth the way back into Parliament and, ultimately, bankruptcy, would later all conspire to cloud young Henry's relationship with his father and acrimoniously prompt him to put his own father onto a corseted financial regime in order to try salvaging the unravelling family accounts.

Before marriage, both young Henry and his wife had each enjoyed the typical upbringing of the well born in the mid-1800s. There were endless gatherings of and visits to friends and relatives. There were dreamy horse and carriage excursions through the rolling southern English countryside. There was a rigorous education at Harrow School as a young man followed by Cambridge. For Henry, home, after Writtle, came to mean the pillared four-story mansion at 4 Chesham Street in London's fashionable Belgravia. The Oxford and Cambridge Club was where he socialised. Or otherwise at the Reform Club. And for variety, Hardcastle père liked taking rented estates in the countryside for a change of scenery. The Norfolk area was a particular favourite. For Maria Sophia, meanwhile, home unequivocally meant Collingwood where she became an accomplished watercolourist, producing fine landscapes and many of the elaborate family holiday cards at Christmas time. It was also where she perfected her language skills and musical talents.

The Herschels and the Hardcastles met early on at Hawkhurst. If Joseph Alfred liked taking his family off to the much-loved Norfolk, particularly to Sheringham and Cromer to the north, he *also* found the beauty of Kent to his taste. Conveniently, there were relatives and a gracious home called Lillesden owned by the extended clan, where they could come for holidays. Not far from Collingwood, it was simply a matter of time, as neighbours from the same milieu, before chemistry between Henry and Maria Sophia

*Chapter 3*

began to work. They belonged to the same social set. There was the proximity of the two homes. *And* there was already one marriage in the pipeline about to unite the two families that took place a year before Alexander's parents wed. It was between Anne Emma Haldane Hardcastle (a step-sister to Henry's father Joseph Alfred) and William James Herschel, Maria Sophia's brother.

*Henry Hardcastle (Courtesy of D.H. Perceval)*

The engagement of our two was probably fairly short for those times. In mid-October 1865, they took their vows at the Hawkhurst Church, scarcely four months after the death of Henry's mother Frances. Thirty-five days later, they were off to Rome. The young bride took her easel and her brushes and set to putting The Eternal City's autumnal scenery down in colour. They called on friends and acquaintances. They toured the classical sites in the outlying *campagna*. And Maria Sophia, off in a contented world of her own, painted, painted, painted. All too soon though, as the winter chill settled in on Italy, it was time to return north, to home. Or rather, to their homes. Those early days of married life were spent moving restlessly between various parental havens. There was Writtle and its magnificent mansions, where Henry took up the reins of the brewery and invested in local pubs. There was the grand Collingwood. And there was 4

Chesham Street, no less splendid, in Belgravia. Their first child Frances, conceived on the eve of their departure from Rome, was already on the way. She was born at Writtle in August 1866. A year later, followed Alice Louise Beatrice, nicknamed 'Beattie'. She, too, came into the world at Writtle. The very next summer, August 27 1868, the couple produced their third child. It was a boy who they named after Henry's father: Joseph Alfred Hardcastle II. Perhaps the name was chosen in part as a 'peace offering' of son to father, burying the hatchet, after many years of strained relations. The *accouchement* took place at Nether Hall in Pakenham, an estate owned by Henry's father with his second wife. There was a brief pause in progeny before the pregnancies resumed. Next came John Herschel Hardcastle, 'Johnny', in 1870, followed by another baby daughter, Mira Francisca in May 1871. These two were also born on their grandfather's country estate at Pakenham. Alexander, or 'Alick', came onto the scene October 25, 1872, born, however, at the Belgravia home in Chesham Street. He and his eldest sister Frances were the only siblings to be single-named on the birth registry. All the others featured two or more names to their credit. Henry Robert – 'Harry' to his family – arrived twenty-four months after Alexander, there in London. The very last Hardcastle child, Henry and Maria Sophia's eighth, was Eleanor Constance, known as 'Kiddy', born in 1879, also at home in London.

*Maria Sophia Hardcastle (Courtesy of D.H. Perceval)*

## Chapter 3

Five years after Alexander's birth, a landmark of a different sort took place. Queen Victoria was made Empress of India. It was a reminder to the world, if one were actually needed, of Britain's might and of its influence throughout the world. The Empire, after all, numbered 372 million people under its umbrella. It held sway over 25 percent of the globe. Its British subjects were to be treated accordingly and the ripples would be felt by this child in his later life.

Although he was busy in town, the ties with Writtle were still strong enough that in 1881, Henry presented a large handsome gold and black clock to the town, which still sits atop the stone tower of All Saints Church there. Later on in life, Joseph Alfred II jotted down some of his childhood memories of Chesham Street:

> I have a vague recollection of the great privilege of being allowed to carry the wine that Papa got out of the cellar each evening, always in two hands, climbing carefully up the stone steps from the basement where bottles were stored.

He also remembered that the children's weekend diversions outside London included 'shooting, picnics, walks around Collingwood, bicycling and collecting butterflies'. And perhaps a little star gazing, in homage to their grandparent.

That sizeable troop of youngsters meant that Henry and Maria had to start thinking of a place somewhat larger. Belgravia was elegant and it was central. Relatives were thickly scattered nearby. Henry began to fix his sights on Eaton Square, scarcely three blocks away. His own sister's in-laws owned property there, at 101 and later, at 104. Designed and built by 'Master Builder' Thomas Cubitt over the 29 years from 1826 to 1855, Eaton Square was, in fact, a rather stretched out rectangle, intersected west to east by the King's Road. A long row of elegant pillared homes, each several stories high began to rise on both sides of the King's Road, with gated greenery to follow, neatly sandwiched in between. Two Doric columns framed the entranceway to each home and gave support to first-story balconies with stuccoed balusters. Rich property-seekers were swift to pounce on this coveted address.

Twelve months after ground-break, William Henry Whitbread, the brewer, crossed the threshold of the very first completed house there. That same year, 1827, St. Peter's Church, with its six fluted columns in front, was consecrated at the east end of the Square, ready to tend to the spiritual needs of its affluent new parish. Before long, consolidating the tone of what was to become London's best postcode, a son of King William IV moved in, as did the Austrian statesman Prince Metternich, American philanthropist George Peabody, two foreign embassies and, later on, two future prime ministers, Stanley Baldwin and Neville Chamberlain.

Number 38 Eaton Square, midway through the rectangle on the south side, was owned during the late 1870s by one Major John Ferguson. In 1882, however, he sold on to Hardcastle. Henry and Maria Sophia and their family of eight swept through the doors, at last in a roomy home truly of their own, where all could spread out. A large grey cat joined the ménage, padding silently up and down the staircase, an integral part of the family. A dog called Dingaan came into the household later on. The wide-eyed, ten-year old Alexander was no doubt agog at the gigantic rooms and high ceilings, echoing under foot, which henceforth were his playgrounds. They gave him his first real conscious taste for the sort of solid surroundings that he would consider his natural birthright later on in life.

*Group photograph* ca. *1882 with unidentified relatives.*
*In the dark suits, left, Henry Robert, 2nd right, Alexander.*
*(Courtesy of D.H. Perceval)*

## –4–

Thirty days short of his fourteenth birthday, Alexander left the comfort and security of 38 Eaton Square to climb the steep rise of Harrow-on-the-Hill, just to the northwest of central London, to enter Harrow School. It was September 1886 and he was still very much a child. Vestiges of baby fat rounded his cheeks. A thatch of fair coloured brows eaved over his brown eyes and a trim crop of curly dark hair, parted on the side, framed his very handsome young face. In photographs he looks a bit ill-at-ease dressed in his clunky woollen suit, starched white collar and watch fob draped across his small chest. Packaged as an adult when he so clearly was not.

In almost turnstile fashion, he was entering Harrow just as his older, look-alike brother Joseph Alfred was exiting. And both, in turn, were following in the path of their father Henry, an Old Harrovian like many of their other male relatives. It was virtually a given that Alexander would follow in their collective footsteps and that he would go through the doors – as they too had done – of one of the most prized houses of them all, The Grove.

Harrow School was founded in 1572. Over the centuries, it weathered periodic ups and downs, notably in the quantity of new students. Eventually, it gained momentum in stature and in prestige. Historian Christopher Tyerman described it as becoming 'synonymous with class, social division and privileged education. [It] remains common shorthand for a certain sort of exclusivity'. In Alexander's day, the only other school its equal was nearby Eton, where his maternal grandfather had put in a brief appearance some eight decades earlier.

In the 1880s, Harrow counted 17 houses large and small where students boarded. They were all privately owned and managed. Their reputations were in good measure shaped by the house masters running them, who were expected to lend firm guidance to their young charges, impart strong moral behaviour and … keep them in line. The Grove met all those criteria and the Hardcastle men felt quite at ease there. It had come – albeit loosely – into the Harrow fold in 1819 when Reverend Samuel E. Batten had purchased the large building sitting somewhat apart from the main aggregation, just below the Church of St. Mary. After a bad fire early in 1833, The Grove had had to be rebuilt from scratch only salvaging the handsome grey façade that it still features today, three stories high, surrounded by stately plantings. If it had boasted a modicum of comfort and frills, that would soon all change, scarcely five years before Alexander's arrival.

In 1881, Edward E. Bowen stepped in as house master and promptly set about reconfiguring the interiors. He decreed that henceforth his young charges should all have separate bedrooms. Indeed, it was the very first house in all of Harrow School to feature single quarters for most of the students. He introduced more substantial breakfasts for his youngsters, to get them off to a better start in the day. Because of his vigilant nature, he was given the nickname 'Sleuth'. Bowen, not much of a cosseter, did not believe in going further overboard. He was very much an outdoors man himself who believed in the benefits of open-air sports and exercise. He had walked the perimeter of England and he expected similar athletic zeal from the boys. Of indoor frills, he took a decidedly dim view, attempting, perhaps fruitlessly, to seed similar inclinations amongst his charges. Baths were anything but warm. The bedrooms were all small and the furnishings sort of tired. Decorative mantelpiece *objets* were frowned upon. Armchairs were deemed downright 'later Roman', that is, decadent. Wooden floors were kept free of carpets and curtains were non-existent. All stuff that was injurious to character, Bowen felt, as was warmth. The heating was asthmatic, to put it charitably. Use of coal fires, in fact, was trimmed back in the Bowen reign, lit up later at night and snuffed out earlier in the morning. In fact, one of Alexander's housemates wrote home telling his parents how he had had to approach Bowen to ask permission to warm his chilled limbs in the master's study. In short, students soon had had to learn to cope with Bowen's personal approach, or rather non-approach, to creature comforts. One light touch was Bowen's talent as a song writer. His 'Forty Years On', written in 1872, became one of the most famous of all school songs.

But there were loftier compensations, of course. Students could count on receiving some of the finest, most rigorous education going. The rarefied environment 400 feet high up on that hill, set so physically far apart from the rest of humanity, ensured that one and all would concentrate better on the business of learning. And much of that took place in architecturally inspiring buildings. There was the magnificent amphitheatre-like Speech Room, richly panelled and pillared, with its gothicky flourishes. It was there that boys assembled every Monday morning for assorted weekly announcements and where important speeches, lectures, plays and ceremonies took place throughout the rest of the year. The stately Vaughan Library on High Street with its elaborate brick-patterned façade was built expressly for Harrow students. Light streamed through its stained-glass windows onto the tables where they read in churchly silence. Further afield was one of Europe's largest swimming pools, 500 feet long, where the boys went for a once-weekly plunge. They called it 'Ducker' because it had been constructed directly over a former duck pond.

But most important of all, Harrow students like Alexander could reckon on being taught by many of the most brilliant minds of the era, alongside those sternly shepherding tendencies of Mr Edward E. Bowen. Such teaching had trained eight British prime ministers, including Sir Winston Churchill in more recent times. Lord Byron studied there, as had Anthony Trollope, William Henry Fox Talbot, Richard Sheridan, Jawaharlal Nehru, King Hussein of Jordan and many distinguished others. The occasional Persian, Zanzibari or Egyptian student, too, gave Harrow a 'cosmopolitan tincture'.

*Chapter 4*

*Joseph Alfred Hardcastle, taken ca. 1882-6, at Harrow School.*
*(By permission of Harrow School Archive)*

By December 1886, barely four months after his arrival, Alexander was already showing signs of his academic mettle, coming out top in a class of fifteen in natural science, while placing second in mathematics. His older brother had shown a similar flair for maths and languages, scooping up prizes along the way. In a letter home to his parents from Harrow, Joseph Alfred, aged 16, gave an inkling of the curricular challenges that lay in store further ahead for his younger brother. In it he wrote:

> Our subjects this term are in Scripture, The Epistles of St Paul, which we do on Sunday afternoons, in order to explain his travels which we do in French ... on Monday mornings. In pupil-room we do Juvenal's Satires, and I ... have begun Gibbon too for Pupil Room. In Latin we are doing Livy. It's very easy ... we go on with Mommsen's History of Rome. In French, we do Thiers, we are doing the

Egyptian Campaign this term. In Natural Science the subject is still Electricity ... . In history we have come to the Reformation, so we have to read innumerable books on it ... . I have to read my Life and Letters of Macaulay and there's any amount of stuff to be prepared for the Scholarships at the end of term ... . I mean to go out running 2 or 3 times a week ... we are doing Botany, it is very interesting ... .

Attendance in the classroom followed a strict dress code and over the years, much has been written about the very characteristic attire. Alexander's brother tuned in with his own recollections:

The clothes we wore at Harrow were singularly inappropriate. All boys below the 5th form wore Eton jackets which afford very little warmth over the parts of the body which require it most ... on our heads we wore very flat straw hats with an elastic which went behind the head and left a tell-tale ridge in the hair of every Harrow boy.

Life at the school, though, was not wholly leaden. Nor were the 'hardships' truly unbearable. There were light – even comic – moments in store. Seven months after his own arrival, in fact, Alexander was to gain a very special fellow housemate among the contingent of forty there, in the form of Gerald Hubert Edward Busson Du Maurier, aged 14, from Hampstead. His Grove mates gathered around to inspect 'the child of fame'. He was the son of a well known Punch Magazine cartoonist, George Du Maurier, much in the limelight in his day. Young Gerald would go on as an adult to become a noted West End theatre manager and matinée idol famed for starring in such plays as 'Dear Brutus', 'Diplomacy' and 'London Pride'. But for the time being, he relished centre stage just about as much as his father, there at The Grove, playing to a captive audience of minors. If Alexander's Herschel genes and taste for hard work were beginning to show, then Gerald's inclinations were heading in another direction. His daughter, author Daphne Du Maurier, remembered from the drift of Gerald's surviving letters to the home front and from the handed-down family stories, that his acting talents were already beginning to show. 'At school, his chief claim to fame was that ... he used to imitate Sir Henry Irving [the noted stage manager] walking up and down the corridors, and the masters and boys used to laugh.' Author James Harding who wrote a biography of Gerald ('Gerald du Maurier. A Biography. The Last Actor-Manager') added:

His charm which he had early learned to manipulate with skill, eased him out of many a difficult situation, and his gift of mimicry transformed annoyance or dislike into sympathetic laughter.

The Du Maurier letters back to Hampstead from Harrow invariably were apologising to Mummy for having done poorly in his studies ... 'some of the things are very hard to understand'... and vowing to do better. A great number were written asking for 'tin' (money) and delicacies like jams, bread and sardines to be dispatched from home. It is not hard to see why. One of his stream-of-consciousness notes, untarnished by good spelling or proper grammar, read:

> Wednesday April 29, 1887  Darling Mummy, We had such a fearful pudding to day [sic] that I hide [sic] it all with my spoon & I then winked at John & he took it away, I will tell you what it was, it was made of blomonge [sic] & plums, literally, bad clotted cream & small black beetles; Mr Walker looked at it as if he meant to say that it was a 'manifestation of insanity'.

Hence the gratitude and persistent pleas for yet more

> roast duck, one or two roll [sic] tongues a big tin of toast and milk apricot, greengage & lots of narbonne [a rich sauce] in glasses not pots & chocolate, etc. ... . I got the cakes which were very good.

When he wasn't busy ordering up care packages from his mother, Du Maurier's correspondence with home might have been that of any of his school friends. On November 12, 1887, the boys were marched in for a sermon. 'Canon Mason, I suppose you've heard of him preached, he is rather a moaning old goat', reported Gerald. And of a noteworthy talk at Harrow he wrote,

> Lord Wolsey [sic] came down on Friday night & gave us a lecture upon the red river expedition, which he commanded.[1] Which he ended up with a short speech on the English gentleman ... whom he hoped would never change, & was very 'The Queen, God bless her'.

Boys from The Grove in that period also got to hear another far more intriguing recruit brought to the Harrow podium. He was Colonel George E. Gouraud, an American Civil War hero of French descent, who had recently won the right to act as inventor Thomas Alva Edison's European agent for the phonograph. He brought the 'new, improved device' for the awed boys to hear. Alexander was there, but it was Gerald who faithfully wrote down on November 18, 1888, one of his many unbridled accounts for Hampstead.

> Colonel Gouraud came on Saturday evening and gave us a lecture on the 'phonograph' & made the thing speak; I never heard any thing so frightfully perfect in my life. Edison had sent over a swell band, bottled up in it & it sounded ripping & at the end, a little voice said, 'Three cheers for the United States,' and we heard all the cheers ... . At the end of the lecture we cheered Edison and sung the last verse of **40 years on** [that school song of Bowen's] which were bottled up, and is going to be sent to Edison. It will probably blow him out of his room.

---

[1] As Colonel Garnet Wolseley, he was dispatched in 1870 from Toronto on the arduous Red River expedition to suppress a rebellion.

Perhaps it was Alexander, who was known to carry around a looking glass, to lend him a Herschel pocket telescope one day during a fit of homesickness. Gerald would write, 'I saw all the people on Hampstead Heath to day, as a chap has a very powerful telescope, but I didn't see any of you.'

*Alexander Hardcastle, taken ca. 1886-90, at Harrow School.*
*(By permission of Harrow School Archive)*

If Hardcastle wrote home to his parents, none of the letters survive. It is assumed that, coming from far less bohemian stock than the likes of Du Maurier, his family expected him to knuckle down and study. The school magazine, The Harrovian, faithfully reported all sporting events, but Alexander's name very rarely appeared there as a team member, save for having played racquets and participated in a tug-of-war event. Nor does he feature as one of the contributors to the publication. Or as an enthusiast of

*Chapter 4*

amateur theatricals. Most likely, the young teenager was glued to his studies. That was in the Herschel tradition and he was no exception in his diligence.

During Alexander's first twenty-four months at Harrow, most of his siblings were also taken up with their respective pursuits. Joseph Alfred – soon to be struck with tuberculosis – had completed a year at Trinity College, Cambridge and moved on, briefly, to try a career in business, while Frances was gearing up with private tutoring to qualify for Girton College, Cambridge, which she entered in 1888. The beautiful Beatrice meanwhile, aged 19, followed her mother's artistic bent, studying as a water colourist and dabbling in comparative religions. Between 1882 and 1887, John attended the Haileybury School, which had opened scarcely twenty years earlier at Hertford. On his departure, he was poised to become a gentleman cadet in the Royal Artillery. Mira Francisca was fifteen when Alexander set off for Harrow. Henry, twelve, prepared to enter Haileybury, like his brother John, in 1887. Little Constance Eleanor, aged seven, was still too young for any of this.

Before too long, Alexander enjoyed a further measure of acceptance within The Grove group. Following a long Harrow tradition, his full name was neatly carved onto a 6 ½ -foot long polished slab of stained oak and mounted on the indoor wall of the house, alongside the names of other young school mates. And there it remains, even today.

In April 1889, The Times was reporting some of the scholastic achievements from the school: 'the results of the examination for scholarships and prizes have been announced. The following candidates were selected … Ponsonby [Bessborough] Modern Scholarship was awarded to A. Hardcastle … the second prize for mathematics to A. Hardcastle.' By Easter 1890, after earning a further accolade, the Neeld Medal for mathematics, Alexander had completed his studies there. It was time to move on. As it was for his brother John, the arrow pointed towards a military career. On the far eastern side of London, a world away from Harrow, stood a large, brooding stone complex. The Shop. That would be the next stop on Alexander's trajectory.

# –5–

Unlike the hilly and tree-shaded preserve of Harrow, Woolwich, nine miles to the east of central London, was a marshy flatland, close to the Thames. It was a no-man's land, really, bereft of charm or softness. In the early days, it had been known as having been the general area where captured pirates were strung up at the gallows, far from prying eyes. The area later came into prominence for its Royal Dockyards.

On July 27, 1890, The Times reported the next event in young Hardcastle's life that had him dispatched off to these forlorn parts:

> The following are declared by the Civil Service Commissioners to have obtained the first 60 places at the examination held in June and July 1890 for admission ... [including] Hardcastle, Alexander.

Alick, in short, had successfully passed the competitive written examination to enter The Shop. He was 17 years, 10 months and one day old, as the military records so meticulously put it. The day of his formal appointment was August 26, 1890. As with Harrow, his parents would be footing his two-year tuition fees, board and uniforms. The investment, they reckoned, was money well spent: as a future engineering officer, career prospects would be promising, appointments interesting, the salary comfortable. He had scarcely a month of freedom to enjoy the final snippets of the English summer with his family at 38 Eaton Square. In 31 days, he would head off to The Shop at Woolwich. Its real name as far as he was concerned was, of course, the Royal Military Academy.

What propelled him into a military career and into the Royal Engineers in particular? It is all conjecture, for he left no explanations behind. Perhaps his brilliance in mathematics made it seem a short stepping stone into engineering. And the military would have assured him of an orderly, regulated life. Maybe engineering skills would serve him well in the years after the military chapter came to a close. He had one uncle on his mother's side, Col. John Herschel, who had served with the Royal Engineers. Had this man put in a good word for his nephew? A further supposition is, quite simply, that that was the accepted norm in large Victorian families: one or more sons *would* land up in the military or in the clergy, assisted, no doubt, by a firm nudge from the parents. If that is the case, then the Hardcastles were true to form.

By then, the Academy was already nearly a century and a half old. Its job was to produce officers for the Artillery and the Engineers. The vast frontage at Woolwich was flanked by large, brooding buildings faced in traditional Welsh slate. The parapets were edged with a flourish of castellation. Coming through the doors that year were 121 fresh-faced gentlemen cadets just like him. Among them was a grandson of the Prime Minister of Madagascar. Less exotic but far more pertinent to the young men's lives was another newcomer: Major-General W. Stirling, the new governor of the Royal Military Academy. He would reign in the top slot throughout the brief years of Alexander's stay there.

As a fourth-class entrant, barrack life on the lowest rung of the ladder was cramped for a newcomer. Indeed the days of a Harrow room all to himself now seemed but a dim memory for Hardcastle! As many as 70 cadets crowded into a classroom at a time for lectures. At the outset, some of the courses were shared with the artillery trainees. 'Bifurcation' later separated the specialities into two distinct entities. Future gunners, it was reckoned, did not need to learn so much about fortifications and mathematics. Equally, engineers – or sappers as they were familiarly called – hadn't to overextend themselves on the ins and outs of riflery. With time, Alexander's courses included not only mathematics and fortifications, but also military topography, tactics, landscape drawing, chemistry and French. The goal was to master the techniques of bridge-building, demolitions, field defences, road building or repair – in short, to learn the methods of helping one's own army move forward and impeding the advance of the enemy. Some of those disciplines would return to help him in Italy years later.

The tempo of life outside the classroom settled into a regular and predictable pattern. After the early morning wakeup bell came breakfast at 7:00 a.m. One sapper described the fare as being 'of a meagre description'. Dinner appeared at 3:00 p.m. It was depicted as: 'consisting of a joint and a very heavy duff [a boiled pudding or dumpling]. Often meat ran short, and when more was required, it was left to the discretion of the officer on duty. Coffee ... of an inferior description at 4:00 p.m. Tea squads at 8:00 – tea of a light shade, loaf of bread and a pat of butter. Sometimes a scanty slice of meat or two bad eggs and on grand occasions a slice of Bologna sausage!'

During moments of leisure, the cadets could read in the richly-panelled library, use the bowling alley and billiard room or otherwise burn off energy on the Academy's cricket pitch. A bit of secret gambling, too, went on, in dress rehearsal for adulthood.

Young Hardcastle moved up the ladder, graduating by the spring of 1891 to the third class, then moved formally into the engineering division of the Royal Military Academy on September 23, 1891. Meanwhile, his headstrong brother John, two years his senior, who also chose the military path, was moving into his first marriage in January 1892. He was scarcely 21 and his wife, Gertrude Lillian Chalice, of Sussex, only 22. Before long, they were off to Malta on posting and it was there that the unfortunate Gertrude died, childless, scarcely 24 months later.

During one break at home in that period, all the Hardcastle children, save John, assembled under the family roof to be fingerprinted. Alexander too, aged 19, submitted to the ink pad. Perhaps it was inspired by their uncle, Sir William James Herschel. He was an early champion of fingerprinting as a technique of personal identification. Fingerprinting had been around for centuries, starting with the Chinese and Japanese. Their uncle had experimented and used it as a sure-fire system of binding workers in

India to their contracts in the 1860s when he was serving there as a government administrator. A Scottish missionary, quite independently, was also experimenting with it as a technique shortly after Herschel, off in Japan. Back in England, polymath Francis Galton, too, fell for the new-fangled rage. Eventually, New Scotland Yard in 1901 adopted fingerprinting as the most effective method of the times for criminal identification. Whatever the inspiration, the Hardcastle children complied eagerly and the careful imprints still survive today.

*Second-lieutenant Alexander Hardcastle, aged 20, in the Corps of the Royal Engineers, Chatham. (Courtesy of the Royal Engineers Museum and Library, Chatham)*

By July 1892, all the hurdles at Woolwich were behind him and Alexander was now '19 years, 8 months and 26 days old'. The peach fuzz on his serious young face had long vanished. His voice deepened and the very first shy hint of a moustache cast its pale outline over his upper lip. Unlike the grown-up suit he posed in for the Harrow photograph, now he looked entirely convincing in his svelte frog-buttoned engineer's jacket and smart sappers' kepi-like cap a-tilt on his head. After two months' leave over the summer of 1892, second-lieutenant Alexander Hardcastle was now officially commissioned as a member of the Corps of the Royal Engineers. From Woolwich, it was a short hop down the road, eastwards, to Chatham and into the School of Military Engineering. By then, his younger brother Henry had graduated from Haileybury and had moved on to Trinity College, Cambridge. His sister Frances, meanwhile, was on course to become a mathematician. Following private education, she had entered Girton College, Cambridge in 1888, very much in the footsteps of her aunt Constance Anne Herschel, Lady Lubbock, who had been a lecturer there in mathematics and natural sciences. Frances then moved on to the United States as a graduate student at Bryn Mawr in 1892. She was appointed an honorary fellow in mathematics at Chicago University and held a further fellowship in mathematics the year after, back at Bryn Mawr. Frances seemingly travelled a lot during her American stay, welcomed by academics and new-made friends in New York, Washington and elsewhere. No matter how far away she was, she always seemed hungry for news from home. In a letter to her mother dated January 18th, 1893 from Bryn Mawr, she wrote:

> I am pleased that Beatrice has written at last, I really believe she is recovering 'tone' mentally and physically but eccentric she will be to the end of the chapter. I mean to write to Harry very soon and gently hint a few pieces of sound advice – but tell Papa if he values Harry's future at all, not to shout over his not working tho' for your own consolation, I may tell you that an <u>average</u> (which is very different from a <u>maximum</u>) of four hours a day is not so very bad for a (Trinity) freshman … . If you could forward one of Johnny's letters I should be grateful, also one of Alfred's – I should like to hear their news and have not written to either of them myself for so long that I know I don't deserve a direct letter – Beside, Johnny only writes to me when he wants me to do something for him and that is not so possible now!

If Alexander had written to her at this moment, he no doubt would have reported that he had completed his final *perfezionamento* at Chatham and that it had lasted thirty-six months **and** that at last he was shipping out with the 41st (Fortress) Company at the end of January 1895 for the Straits Settlements in the Far East.

A British crown colony for only the previous twenty-eight years, the Straits Settlements consisted in a sizeable agglomerate of land and islands along the southern and western parts of the Malay Peninsula, including Penang and the brightest jewel of it all, Singapore. Its most important raison d'être was to service Britain's trade with China. In the not-too-distant decades before, however, the tectonic plates of politics had crunched unsettlingly upon one another in various corners of the world, causing old alliances to shift, new enmities to rise. The Indian Mutiny of 1857-58 drove home to the English how dangerously fast an uprising could spread, threatening British hegemony. In the mid-1880s, the expanding new French protectorate in Indochina cast its own shadow over the status quo in Asia. At about the same time, another crisis flared up when Russian troops clashed with Afghan soldiers and annexed the Pendjen Oasis, bringing

Britain to the edge of another crisis. Sufficient political reasons then for Britain to further strengthen its foothold in the Settlements.

*On the steps of the barracks at Chatham. '2nd Lieut. Vickers' Batch, joined July 22, 1892. (Courtesy of the Royal Engineers Museum and Library, Chatham)*

But economic considerations, too, counted in no small part alongside politics. This thriving Anglo-Asian preserve depended heavily on the benefits of shipping traffic. The opening of the Suez Canal in 1869 had greatly shortened the voyage to the East. More and more vessels were steaming through the Malacca Straits and on into the Pacific. Calling in, of course, at Singapore. The aim, as James Morris put it in 'Pax Britannica – The Climax of an Empire' was that 'Everywhere British ships could berth in British harbours, stock up with British coal, replenish their supplies of British beer or biscuits, paint their hulls with British paint, pick up their instructions from British cable stations beneath the protection of British guns'. In short, that route *had* to be assured. The sticking point was <u>who</u> was going to pay for the envisaged reinforcement of the defences: London or Singapore? Like the disagreeable hot potato that it was, the problem got bounced back and forth. In the end, Britain grudgingly made noises that they would pay up and with that, the work began, to build up Singapore's port area and to construct new barracks and other military facilities. Thirty-six months later, one of the many islands just south of Keppel Harbour, three miles from the centre of town, was made into a navy and military base. It was called Pulau Brani, which meant Island of the Brave in Malay. It was flat, small and conveniently close to the mainland. It was there that the Royal Engineers had their headquarters. Pulau Brani became home to Alexander for the next three years.

*Alexander aged about twenty-one, London. (Courtesy of D.H. Perceval)*

The Singapore of 1895 was a bustling, dynamic and cosmopolitan enclave. In a sense, it was three towns – English, Chinese and Malay, with a population of 140,000. It was particularly idyllic if you were one of the 6000 Europeans. A yacht club, opened in 1881, set the tone, as did the golf club which followed ten years later in 1891. A swimming club followed in 1894, the year before Hardcastle arrived. The famous Raffles Hotel would open later on, in 1899. The official military post report giving guidelines for an appropriate wardrobe to bring out from England hardly smacked of hardship or conflict. 'White dinner jackets ... especially for dances' were suggested. So, too, were riding breeches, a sporting rifle, and light-weight clothing for playing cricket or going out sailing.

At the city's heart was a cacophonous tangle of streets. Rickshaws eeled their way through a maze of bullock carts, road sweepers and private carriages in a picturesque struggle with gridlock. Exotic smells wafted upwards in smoky swirls from roadside braziers, cooks flipping their bright lacquered meats over and over on the coals. Chickens squawked from within their reed-woven cages. Hawkers rasped out the merits of their wares in a patter of Malay, while bony-ribbed dogs barked in a language all of their own. Alongside these colourful sites, too, were immaculate wide boulevards, monumental churches, pristine botanical gardens, social clubs, gracious waterside villas for the rich overlooking a gaggle of bobbing sampans, junks and tongkans. The sights, the sounds, the smells and the steamy tropical heat all told the taciturn 23-year old Hardcastle that he was a long way from the drab, damp greyness of a muffled Chatham winter.

*An undated picture of the trim young officer. (Courtesy of D.H. Perceval)*

A little more than half way through his tour of duty there, on June 22, 1897, a day of pomp was staged throughout the Empire: Queen Victoria and her subjects were marking a sort of colossal 'family reunion' and birthday in honour of her 60 years on the throne. She transmitted a message to her far-flung subjects: 'From the bottom of my heart I thank my beloved people. May God bless them'. A memorable four-hour procession through London took place with colourfully-clothed dignitaries from all her dominions present. This Diamond Jubilee was also celebrated elsewhere in her empire. Medals were struck and monuments unveiled. In Singapore, celebrations actually got a head start with Thanksgiving Services held in the principal churches. A grand ball was held up the hill in Government House and a large Chinese parade snaked its way through town. There were fireworks and illuminations which 'transformed Singapore at night into a fairyland of light'. The garrison at Pulau Brani, too, pulled out all the stops for Victoria.

Back home, meanwhile, life carried on as usual at Eaton Square. Once a week, Alexander's father Henry trotted over to visit with his sister Mary Josephine, Lady Monkswell at her home at 7 Chelsea Embankment, overlooking the Thames. The Chelsea Embankment area had been wrested from the river scarcely twenty-three years earlier. Designed by Sir Joseph Bazalgette, the broad riverside stretch and its gardens had a dual purpose: to give London a useful through road cleverly built to conceal sewage works below and to provide a handsome expanse of greenery, to boot. Before long, it became desirable real estate for home-seekers as well. It was scarcely a 20-minute walk to the southeast from Henry's home to his sister's place. On the afternoon of February 15, 1897, sitting in the parlour with Mary Josephine was another man. The face was only vaguely familiar and his accent even more so. But the unruly thicket of white hair and the droopy moustache should have been a giveaway as to who the illustrious gentleman was: Mark Twain, too, had come for tea.

Time flew and by mid-February 1898, Alexander's Straits posting came to an end. He was now Lieutenant Hardcastle. He was headed back to England, to be stationed at Shorncliffe in Kent.

*Family gathering at 38 Eaton Square ca. 1898. Left to right, front: Maria Sophia, Eleanor, Joseph Alfred, Henry. Back, left to right: Frances, Alexander, Mira Francisca. (Courtesy of D.H. Perceval)*

## –6–

His return to England was a happy time on the family front. Brother John was promoted to captain in the Artillery in mid-March of 1899. There was a welcome break from barrack life one toasty weekend in mid-May up in Eaton Square. Alexander, who was now approaching twenty-seven, linked arms with his sister Eleanor and his mother Maria Sophia to attend early service at St. Peter's Church on Whit Monday, May 22, just down the street from home. Maria Sophia noted in her journal that the very next day, this trio headed up to Marylebone Road to dip into Madame Tussauds Waxworks. 'Alick, Eleanor and I went to Madame Tussauds which I had not seen since '78 or '79 but we found the hot damp crowd too much for our feelings and so did not stay long.' Alexander requested further leave not long after that for another happy family occasion: his adored older brother Joseph Alfred was getting married at Ascot on August 2, 1899 to Theresa Clive Bayley and the groom wanted Alexander to stand as best man. Mira Francisca and Eleanor, resplendent in large white plumed hats and long lacy gowns were among the bridesmaids for Theresa. A wedding photograph under a striped canopy shows the couple with Alexander, now sporting a trim moustache, in his slim-line black tails immediately behind them, staring into the camera. Garlanded around the couple are four bridesmaids and three youngsters doing duty as flower girls and ring bearer. Theresa was thin, angular and kept her dark hair drawn up high on her head. She had something of a jutting chin, a bit to her disadvantage. What she may have lacked in beauty, however, she more than amply made up for in charm and in a talent to write, carefully chronicling for future generations all that occurred around her within the Hardcastle family circle. Last but not least, certainly, she was utterly devoted to her new husband, now suffering from the onset of tuberculosis. Indeed, the newlyweds began their married life in the mild climate of the Italian Riviera, not far from San Remo. Presciently, Alexander gave his new sister-in-law an elegant lace parasol as a wedding gift, the better to shield herself from the Italian sun. One account of the wedding was sent back home by Robert Monkswell to his mother Mary Josephine. In the letter – somewhere between amusement and perplexity, one assumes – he told her of the rather odd behaviour of her own brother Henry, the groom's father. On no account, Henry insisted, was the bridal couple to be showered at the end of the festivities with rice. It had to be *boiled* first! Perhaps it was because he was under a moment of particular stress: his own father, with whom he had that long history of discord, was on his deathbed and indeed would die six days after the wedding. Alexander would make his way from sweetness to sorrow, travelling on from the Ascot wedding to Beaminster in Dorset for the burial of his paternal grandfather, who had caused so much unrest in family relations. Through all of this, Henry's new daughter-in-law bore the family oddities sportingly. Maria Sophia, less so, as we later learn from the records.

*August, 1899: The wedding of Joseph Alfred Hardcastle to Theresa Clive Bayley at Ascot. As best man, Alexander stands between the couple. To the immediate left of Joseph Alfred is his sister Eleanor. To the right of Theresa is Mira Francisca. (Courtesy of D.H. Perceval)*

'We are not interested in the possibilities of defeat; they do not exist', wrote Queen Victoria tersely to the First Lord of the Treasury, Arthur James Balfour in December 1899. She was referring, of course, to the catastrophic 'Black Week' that had just befallen her troops in South Africa.

It was the opening months of the Boer War and Britain had just suffered a terrible trio of defeats at Magersfontein, Stormberg and Colenso with some 7000 casualties. The war had been triggered by England's desire to unite South Africa under Imperial British rule. The two defiant adversaries to that plan were the Boer republics of the Orange Free State and Transvaal which were holding out for their *own* independence. Diamonds and the discovery and exploitation of gold – Transvaal was exporting £24 million in gold that year – were too tempting a treasure to turn one's back on and it was the ill-concealed subtext in this conflict. The stubborn styles of the two opponents did not help either. And thus war was formally declared on October 11, 1899. Within nine days, the very first troopships left Southampton for the 6000-mile voyage to the front. Over the next three years between 1899-1902, 450,000 imperial troops would be deployed to South Africa. At the very outset, Britain overconfidently banked on a speedy dénouement. The two rebellious Boer states thought otherwise. The initial phase of set-piece battles led to 'Black Week'. Boer tactics later would shift to guerrilla warfare.

*Three sisters: Mira Francisca 1871-1959 (top), Frances 1866-1942 (left), Beatrice 1867-1945 (right) taken in 1899. (Courtesy of D.H. Perceval)*

*Chapter 6*

The Queen's strong words to Balfour sent a firm message out: massive military reinforcements were to be dispatched immediately to help redress those December losses. The countdown began for Alexander. From his base at Lydd on the south Kent coast where he was then serving as division officer, he, too, would be off for South Africa before long.

*Summer gathering post 1899. Left to right: Mira Francisca, Alexander, Theresa, Eleanor, Robert Henry. (Courtesy of D.H. Perceval)*

The SS Goorkha stood in the port of Southampton that grey morning of Thursday January 4, 1900, waiting silently for the arrival of its young uniformed passengers off the troop trains coming in from London and Kent. In the course of the Boer War alone, Southampton saw the lion share of men funnelled through that exit point, boarding 400 troopships, together with 27,000 horses. The Goorkha was of recent vintage, having been built in the dockyards of Belfast only three years earlier. Three decks high, with a single smoke stack, weighing 6287 tons, it was owned by the Union-Castle Mail Steamship Company and started out life as a merchant vessel. Now, it had been requisitioned by the Army to carry its forces to war. Captain F.J. Moseley stood out on deck of his ship staring down at the wharf far below, his eyes scanning the crowd for a dignitary soon to arrive. This was his ship's second run in a row to South Africa as a troop transporter. The load would far exceed its intended capacity. No matter. These weren't ordinary times. As the morning wore on, trains began disgorging their passengers. Onto the ship trudged eight horses, along with well over 1250 men. The manifest included the Ninth Field Company of the Royal Engineers. Alick was among them, making his way up the gangplank that morning.

Moseley finally spotted the man he had been waiting for. Smoothing his uniform, checking the angle of his cap, he headed down the steps to greet the Duke of Connaught who had come on board for lunch and to see off the fresh contingent of fighters. When lunch was over, the two men said their farewells and the Duke stepped ashore. With that, the Goorkha hauled anchor, eased slowly away from its berth and headed south towards the English Channel. As the young men leaned on the railings of the portside deck for their final glimpse of home, the Goorkha passed a vast building on the eastern side of Southampton Water. At a full quarter-mile in length, with a grandstand view out to sea and its very own private 558-foot pier, it was unmissable to Alexander. He stared in grim fascination at its brick façade, turrets, belvederes and imposing central dome. Half-knowing what its purpose was. Half not wanting to. In time, hundreds would sadly experience first-hand what stood behind the doors of that enclosed world, as they were brought in from far-flung conflicts, wounded or diseased. It was the Royal Victoria Military Hospital, known simply as Netley. The very largest building of its kind ever built at the time, in the aftermath of the Crimean War. It could accommodate up to 1000 patients at a time. 'Netley' was not a word uttered lightly. Indeed, it sent a shudder down the spines of many. People like Alexander would come to abhor one particular part of that enormous complex. It was the saddest ward of all, hidden from view, referred to only in abbreviated form, as if a fuller name might bring further shame or indignity showering down on the heads of all who were brought there.

By January 9th, the ship had successfully navigated through the uncertain waters of the Bay of Biscay and called in briefly at Tenerife in the Canary Islands for fresh provisions. Then it was off again, headed south. The men drilled by day out on deck and did a bit of target practice. They exercised and ticked days off the calendar. They scanned the horizon for the first signs of land.

Then, finally, on the morning of January 25th, Moseley brought the Goorkha into the Cape Town harbour. Dosia Bagot, the English founder of the Portland Hospital, which she took to South Africa to help nurse the troops, described in her book 'Shadows of the War' what the atmosphere was like:

> Cape Town became like a huge garrison town. Khaki-clad men swarmed in the streets, on the railway, on the trams – khaki, khaki, khaki everywhere. Heavy transport wagons and gun carriages lumbered through the town from the docks to the station, with silent resolute-faced men sitting inside or walking after, the novelty of a strange country failing to arouse in them the slightest trace of outward emotion as they marched doggedly along. Dockyards, by no means too large in times of peace, feebly attempted by day and night to cope with the ever-increasing traffic whilst natives by scores and by hundreds assisted in the unloading of various freights of men and horses and supplies. So the docks resounded … with the ceaseless tramp of thousands of feet, the everlasting rattle of donkey engines swinging cargo ashore, the rolling of trolleys and the banging of horses' hoofs … everyone scrambling through the

## Chapter 6

work, fetching and carrying, uniting in the same feverish struggle to shove everybody and everything forward in a northerly direction – exactly where was of no particular consequence ... one idea alone was paramount with them, that everything was going to strengthen that vast army now marching forward which was to crush the heart out of the man who bore the detested name of 'old Kruger'.

In the first six weeks of the new year, at least 30,000 additional troops disembarked at Cape Town. Throughout January 1900, the railway out of town was largely used to convey provisions to various depots. The Boer War was to witness the first great expansion of the Corps of Royal Engineers in modern times. In due course, among other things, they would control and operate some 4600 miles of railways in South Africa.

The evening of their arrival, Alexander's Company under the command of Major H.J.W. Jerome entrained on the Western Railway for Orange River Station to join the 7th Infantry Division. The journey northeast took two days, chugging past towns with unpronounceable names. On arrival, they marched immediately north to the Maple Leaf Camp where the top priority was to start putting in place improved water supplies for the troops: storage tanks and pumps were promptly set up. On the following days, the Ninth Field Company fanned out on separate forays. Alexander's section marched to Witteput Station to repair roads and drifts (fords) across streams in the area. They also helped build railway sidings in the area.

By February 9th, the Company then edged further into the Orange Free State, nearing Jacobsdal, mending roads as they went. A cache of three tons of enemy dynamite was found and destroyed, as were large quantities of ammunition. By February 20th, Alexander's unit had made its way forward along the south bank of the Modder River; under cover of darkness, deep trenches were dug, pushing nearer and nearer to the Boers' encampment. But by daybreak the next morning, they found themselves opposite the centre of the enemy laager, about 800 yards away and suddenly under heavy fire. Nonetheless, trench work continued, closer and closer. Alexander sat down six days later and wrote to his sister Mira a first-hand account of those momentous days from his own vantage point:

> Camp near Paardeberg,
> 20 miles East of Jacobsdal on Modder
> 27 Feb. 1900

> I have at last arrived at the absolute front & find it much more comfortable than getting there. I got on to the ox wagon (5 to 15 yoke of oxen) with my valise & saddle box at 4 p.m. at Modder, but owing to a wagon being stuck in the drift & wounded coming back from Klipdrift etc. we only got across at 8 a.m. and then waited till 4 o'c before proceeding i.e., 1 mile in 12 hours. Got into Jacobsdal at 9 p.m. At 9 it poured, so being dark, & country unknown, I got under the very greasy & stiff cover of the wagon which squashed me flat against the ammunition boxes under it. Head sticking out over the side, quite impossible position to sleep. But I arose quite dry at 3 a.m. &

strolled round Jacobsdal like a stray dog, found an hotel where a Dutchman still provided meals at moderate prices, his dining room being used as a guard-room by night. He had fed the Boer Officers just the same day before. Old straps, uniforms, broken windows, dead horses etc. everywhere. Three divisions between here and Modder. There are enormous convoys, 200 wagons, i.e. 10 miles nearly – cavalry escorts far out on flanks, laager at night. You 'make good' horses & sheep whenever you see them astray, i.e. convert them to your own use. I came into this camp 2 hours after [General Piet Arnoldus] Cronje hoisted the white flag, & on going to report, saw him & Mrs Cronje meeting [Lord] Roberts. They had a meal at once, & were driven to Modder with 6 R.A. horses. The 4000 prisoners marched, funny looking people, no uniforms, all ages; women & children came out also.

After General Cronje's surrender, Alexander's company helped erect pontooned river crossings where the Boers had blown up the regular bridges. They travelled forward to Bloemfontein with the approach of mid-March, establishing water supplies for the troops, digging troughs, building hospital units, putting up fencing, smoothing roads for easier passage. All work vital to the forward push of the British troops. Then, on May 10$^{th}$ Hardcastle's unit came upon yet another huge cache of Boer matériel that had to be destroyed. Seven hundred thousand rounds of small arms ammunition were set off in a spectacular and noisy conflagration which perhaps was the insidious trigger that would come to haunt him for the rest of his life. 'Something' happened on May 14, 1900. Like a thickly-padded theatre curtain sweeping closed across a stage to shield spectators from the unfolding events in front of them, Lieutenant Hardcastle's South African experience suddenly took a mysterious turn. Matters were hushed up. Closing ranks protectively around their own kind, the Royal Engineers would only tersely note 'On Sick Leave' in their official Statement of Services.

Anticipating severe casualties, the British had outfitted ten hospital ships to carry the gravely wounded or sick home, while the lighter casualties were treated in field hospitals locally. By the close of the war, between 5000-6000 of the British military died on the battlefield. Another some 15,000 succumbed to disease – enteric fever, typhoid, being the major killer. Alexander's troubles, however, were of a very different nature. His sister-in-law Theresa gave only a very veiled hint when she wrote, in her account of the Hardcastle family, that Maria Sophia 'had great courage in facing the manifold difficulties of her life'. Having known the history surrounding the delicate mental health of her own father and grandfather, Maria Sophia would have recognized what was now happening to her very own son. This tragic illness which had so unspooled members of her family in the past was now directly on her doorstep maybe caused by the incessant explosions he had heard in South Africa. Many, many decades later, in November 1982, Alexander's beloved niece Felicité Hardcastle, to whom he was godparent, came clean in a very candid letter that she wrote to another relative: '[Alexander] joined the R.E. ... then had a nervous breakdown ... .'

In the shipping news pages of The Times, Alexander was reported as leaving South Africa on June 9$^{th}$, 1900, aboard **HMHS Maine.** With him were another 148 among the sick, wounded or convalescing. On loan from America's Atlantic Transport Line, this vessel was described as 'the most complete and comfortable hospital ship that has ever been constructed'. Thirty days later, on Wednesday July 4th, Alick was back on English soil.

As the largest place of its kind, many soldiers invalided out of South Africa from the Boer War were brought back to Netley. Others were parcelled out to the Herbert Hospital at Woolwich which could take 600 patients or to the Cambridge Military Hospital at Aldershot with its 800 beds. But Netley had additional facilities that others did not readily have. With its 138 wards, this Southampton hospital had been formally inaugurated in 1863. But a further, less-publicized adjunct had quietly opened seven years later, in July 1870, elsewhere on the grounds. It was two stories high and constructed in yellow and red brick. And it was sited where no one could properly see it from the outside. One author who has written about this military hospital, Philip Hoare, suggests that perhaps that was where the flip phrase 'around the bend' comes from, because the Military Lunatic Asylum was indeed concealed from sight, behind the corner of Netley's principal building. The Asylum – which actually encompassed two buildings – became known simply as 'D Block' and 'E Block' and everyone knew what that meant. During the period of October 1899 to May 1902, there were 640 admissions for mental disease amongst troops serving in South Africa.

Whether he was actually sent there initially or not isn't known. If he followed the pattern of his two Herschel ancestors – and he probably did – there was no evidence of violent behaviour. Some military-medical histories suggest that victims of what would later be termed as shellshock who posed no danger to those around them were quietly released into the care of their own families. Thus it is quite possible that Henry and Maria Sophia at least at the outset swept him into the protective folds of 38 Eaton Square. As a serving member of London's Metropolitan Asylums Board, his father was attuned to the tragedies of the mentally disturbed. Alexander's parents would nurse him as best they knew.

# –7–

Maria Sophia was increasingly nursemaid to more than just her own son. Theresa did not mince words in her journal when she described the household situation:

> [Henry Hardcastle was] a strange man clever and kind, but very delicate and devoid of any sense of responsibility – leaving everything difficult to be done to his wife and his daughters Frances and Mira and to Alfred … . She was … quite out of her métier as wife of a very morose, delicate man … her family of four sons and four daughters were I think more a source of trouble and anxiety than a joy to her … . [She] had great courage in facing the manifold difficulties of her life and was most loyal to her husband, whose fear of responsibility always made him throw everything on her to do and decide. The consequence was that she was very reserved – and undoubtedly somewhat hard – her mind very much of a Presbyterian monk.

Adding to the burdens already on her shoulders was also the matter of lopsided backgrounds. Maria Sophia's early family life under the Herschel roof was imbued with love and warmth. The behaviour of Henry's father, instead, had stirred strains and mistrust in his son and no doubt inspired Henry's instinct to eschew commitment. These differences surely must have impacted on their coexistence at 38 Eaton Square.

Slowly, Alexander *did* mend. For action at Dreifontein in South Africa, he was awarded the Queen's Medal with two clasps, blunting some of the perceived shame of his breakdown. To fill out the days of sick leave, there were family events to keep him distracted. Events in the public domain, too, were grabbing people's attention. On a bitterly cold January day of 1901, Queen Victoria died at Osborne House, her Isle of Wight residence. She had reigned for nearly 64 years and a pall rolled over the nation like thick fog, as the news spread from town to town. Church bells tolled, actors walked off stage in mid-performance and people huddled publicly for further news. In the textile mills of the north, looms weaving brightly-coloured fabrics came to an abrupt halt, re-gearing for bereavement black. After a short period at Osborne House, her casket was removed to the mainland. From Portsmouth, the funeral train took her to Victoria Station. During that very same time, the Hardcastle family was beginning the countdown to their closing of the Eaton Square property nearby. They would have been quite aware of the solemn proceedings a few blocks away and most probably walked to the station to witness the historic moment. From Victoria Station, the procession, counting four monarchs and six crown princes, made its way north through the hushed streets of London, on through Hyde Park, headed for Paddington Station for the final leg of the journey to Windsor for lying-in-state and burial in early February.

Life carried on in the Hardcastle ménage. Harry began his very brief career in the curacy, first at Henley, later moving on to Selly Oak and Shirley in the Birmingham area. Joseph Alfred, dogged by ill health, bowed out of a brief business career and became a 'free lance' extension lecturer in astronomy, which was his real love. He divided his time between Oxford and Cambridge universities. John, meanwhile, was still in the Royal Artillery, soon to retire. Already he was devoting much of his time to perfecting rifle design. It was also around this time that Henry and Maria Sophia decided to pull up stakes altogether from London. By then, he was 65 years old and his wife, 66. Between 1901 when they sold Eaton Square and 1905 when they purchased a property in greater Oxted (Surrey), there was no one real Hardcastle base. As on other occasions, they followed the accepted practice of renting properties as they saw fit or otherwise descending on their many relatives.

The countryside eventually drew them in when they spotted Moor House, a sprawling property at Hurst Green near Oxted, owned by Ernest J. Lovell. It was far larger than London had ever been. The main building was several stories high and was a bit of a rabbit warren within. The attic quarters were spacious enough to accommodate the servants. There were stables and other outbuildings as well, where such retainers as the faithful Hardcastle coachman, Walter Shepherd, could live. A well-laid out pleasure garden, too, was part of the package, as well as 6 ½ acres of land. Furthermore, it was close to the train line into London; travel time into London was scarcely 40 minutes. On February 9, 1905, Moor House became theirs. And it would provide refuge for whichever of their grown children were in need of a place to call home. But Moor House was still four years off in the future.

In September 1901, a huge get-together in Kent was held to mark the golden wedding anniversary of Alexander's great-uncle Edward Hardcastle and his wife Priscilla, four years before Edward's death, aged 75. Remarkably, nearly seventy relatives turned up for the occasion and they all assembled on the sprawling lawn of the family home, New Lodge at Hawkhurst to be captured in a group portrait. Alexander stands in the rear row, staring transfixed at the camera, surrounded by crowds of his family.

The biggest family event of all, though, was an announcement made scarcely two months later: Theresa was pregnant with her and Joseph Alfred's first child. This was cause for particular jubilation because she was the sole standard-bearer for the Hardcastle name. She alone was to give children to the next generation. All of Henry and Maria Sophia's daughters remained spinsters. And of the four sons, only two married – John and Joseph Alfred. None of John's three wives produced an heir. It was thus Theresa to save the day. Her firstborn would be Felicité, born July 1, 1902. The next morning, Alexander ducked into the Elizabeth Street post office in London and dispatched a short but gushing telegram to the new parents: 'Best wishes to heiress of all the ages. Alick.' With good reason he had sent off such a warm wire. He had stood as best man for his older brother and was now chosen godparent. He and Felicité would be bound in fond correspondence in the years to come. Felicité's brother Maurice Alfred Clive Hardcastle, was born twenty-two months later.

*A gathering of the clan. The golden wedding anniversary of Edward and Priscilla Hardcastle in Kent, 1901. Alexander stands in the rear row, seventh from the left, next to Henry Robert. (Courtesy of D.H. Perceval)*

*Chapter 7*

*Henry Robert and Alexander Hardcastle on the occasion of their parents'
golden wedding anniversary, 1915. (Courtesy of D.H. Perceval)*

Alick resumed military service and floated around between bases at Waltham Abbey, Lydd and Chatham. Made captain in 1903, he at last received orders: he was to return once again to South Africa on a final – and calmer – three-year posting, first as District Officer at Bloemfontein, then as Acting Commander at Harrismith and Natal. On July 24, 1907, he retired, still a youthful 34. The next fourteen years, until his departure for Italy, are largely shrouded in mystery. Age prevented him from returning to the military to fight at the outbreak of The Great War. He did, however, take up an unspecified desk job with the military at home to do his part. In 1915, not at the most propitious time in history, his parents marked their golden wedding anniversary. As was the low-key Hardcastle custom, the children posed for photographs to present to their elders.

Just possibly, a more active role in the military was ruled out for another reason: Alexander was struck with a second occurrence of mental illness in 1917, the same year as his brother Joseph Alfred's death, finally felled by the tuberculosis that had cursed him much of his adult life. It was a tragedy in many respects. The older Hardcastle brother had just been appointed to the coveted directorship of the Armagh Astronomical Observatory in Ireland which he had eagerly been looking forward to. He had left his adored Theresa widowed, with two small children. The combined calamity may have played a part in triggering Alexander's second breakdown.

On a brighter note, other matters were in place. By then, his father Henry had made his financial arrangements for the children. Alexander was very comfortably padded for whatever the future held in store. As health was restored, he could now focus on mapping out the coming years. The next chapter could now begin.

## -8-

1920 was the watershed year in Alexander's life. He was now forty-eight years old. Tall and trim, his wavy chestnut hair had now begun to turn grey, ebbing from his wide forehead. The lenses of his metal-rimmed glasses thickened as his eyesight dimmed and his deeply furrowed brow registered the emotional strains of earlier years. The hesitant moustache of his youth, still very dark, was now bushy and pronounced, spread generously across his upper lip. Both the Royal Engineers' career and the Great War were well behind him. His six surviving siblings each had gone off on their respective tangents. Only two of them had married. His parents had long since uprooted from 38 Eaton Square to live at Oxted. He was welcome there, of course. But it was not truly *his*. In short, he was treading water and knew it. If he did not make a decisive move now, perhaps he never would. In early financial settlements made to him by his father in 1895 and 1911, Alexander had already been provided for in the amount of £6300, a very tidy sum in those days – nearly £1 million in terms of today's purchasing power. A sizeable amount was prudently invested. His military pension of £120 was now on stream. He had the wherewithal, in other words, to do precisely whatever he wished. In a place like Sicily, such sums went a very, very long way.

What exactly prompted his move to the southern Mediterranean? It is a matter of guesswork, punctuated with far more question marks than with answers. Did he *know* early on that it would be for good and that he would never again set foot in England? No one quite knows. Did his oldest sister Frances overwhelm him unbearably with her academic prowess and her involvement with the suffragette movement? While his military career was spent between a quiet outpost of Empire, a truncated period in South Africa and assorted desk jobs back home, not to mention his illness, she, Frances, had scooped up both honorary and full fellowships abroad. She had published. There might have been some envy. Equally, had his brother Joseph Alfred – alas, now dead from tuberculosis – cast a long shadow of accomplishment over Alexander with his short but distinguished life as an astronomer? Did these two unwittingly give their brother the sort of inferiority complex that he felt he could only overcome by striking out on his own, to pursue his very own interests? Jealousies and resentments might possibly have played a part.

Two of his relatives shed a ray of faint light on other factors. Theresa, ever the faithful scribe, noted that 'all these eight children were blessed with brains beyond the usual, inherited chiefly from the Herschel side and they were not a loving happy family such as I was accustomed to, and each very much absorbed in their own lives'. Alexander's niece

Felicité homed in even more specifically to a possible fracture between the siblings in a letter to a female relative written in late 1982. Speaking about the two brothers settled in Sicily, she wrote: 'They allowed none of the family to visit them except Mira … .'

His father instinctively felt the simple explanation for his son's decision lay elsewhere. 'Archaeology is very pleasant for you', he told his son over and over. Clearly, he spotted a budding passion for antiquity rising in Alexander. That being so, a move to Sicily seemed entirely natural. It was probably a mixture of all four things: sibling envy, scant attachment to one another, an out-and-out family feud and a growing love for a new subject. But there were even more inspirations to prompt his move.

Intriguing descriptions from the journals and letters sent back home by his Herschel grandfather, Sir John, recounting his voyages of discovery were safely kept by the family and had to have piqued Alexander's curiosity and helped shape his decision. Page after page of the young man's accounts of his travels on the Continent depicted adventurous places that he was seeing. Experiences that were challenging, often uncomfortable, sometimes downright awful. But nonetheless, enriching. Nowhere more so than at the very southern shores of Sicily, nearly 2000 miles from home, where Herschel had travelled to, 96 years before his grandson Alexander. Listen to some of the colourful words Sir John wrote:

Girgenti June 27, 1824

Dear Mother:
… 6 days travelling on mule back over the most desolate country you can conceive has brought us safely to this spot famous for its ruins. The weather is hot – the accommodations infamous and the people <u>lousy</u> excuse the word, for there is no other expressing precisely the fact yet though suffering sadly from these 3 causes I cannot say I regret coming here. The remarkable objects I have met hitherto are Palermo – The ruins of Segesta – Those at Selinunte (where I measured the shaft of one column 31 feet round) – The sulphur mines of Catolica [sic] where I loaded myself with minerals till the muleteer swore it was impossible for the mules to carry them – and here I am. [I believe James[1] fancies] that we have got to the world's end…

Catania July 1, 1824

Dear Mother,
… Hitherto we have succeeded without the slightest material injury or difficulty in every part of my plans. The difficulties of Sicilian travelling of which I had heard so much, are nothing more than what must be encountered in a poor, mountainous country where there are no roads passable for wheeled carriage & where all communication is on foot or on mule back, and the best proof of its perfect security is that we have already travelled over nearly 300 miles of it without being obliged to deviate a single day from our preconcerted arrangement. The climate to be sure is hot but we are now much less sensible to this inconvenience than at entering Sicily … .

---

[1] James Child, his servant.

> The probability of loss & delay will not allow me to enter into any description of the country … . Girgenti is a most curious place & full of ruins, the rocks being all honeycombed with houses etc. and the Temples superb. I have crammed my drawing cases with views of them, which if I do not lose them on my way home will be interesting.

Evidently wearied by some of the local animal life, he commented to his mother in another letter that, 'the mule is the Sicilian nightingale for all its night time braying … .'

Palermo July 16, 1824

> To Sir W. Watson[2]
> … This is indeed a strange country, & to me like a new world … The first impressions of a tropical climate … have a peculiar charm for your inhabitants of a colder region. The cloudless summer skies and glorious sunsets – the deep indigo tint of the clear glassy sea which seems to enjoy a perpetual immunity from … storms would disfigure our ruder element – the intense verdure of the thick orange groves intersected with majestic hedge-rows of tall spiny aloes and impenetrable thickets of enormous cactuses the sunburnt hills and scorched inhabitants with your uncouth jargon – wild expression and half barbarous habits – form a picture that impresses itself on your imagination with a force not to be described – but it is only in chosen, fertile & favoured spots…that nature is thus rich and beautiful – the greater part of the island consists of wild and wastes overgrown with dry thistles and thorny plants where now & then only a sulphureous [sic] and brackish spring makes the scarcity of water more severe & where … pestilential nature … strips the plains of their inhabitants and drives all peasantry of the country to herd in mountain villages and leave the land below a solitude – indeed a desert. In such melancholy solitudes are the principle remains of Sicilian antiquity situated … . The ruins of ancient Agrigentum too stand now far aloof from the modern town which has retreated from the pestilential influence of the air … to the summit of a hill 2 or 3 miles off. It is incredible what an awful air this circumstance gives them. One must be on the spot to feel its full effect.

And afterwards to his close friend and former Cambridge University companion Charles Babbage[3] he wrote:

> I have now made the tour of Sicily and I thank heaven it is done. If it be pleasure to ride from 30 to 50 miles a day over roads all but impracticable for miles under a scorching sun with the thermometer at 86 and over wilds and waste where no verdure is to be seen, but groups of cactus and hedge-rows of majestic aloes from 20 to 30 feet high to break the monotony – to be <u>broiled</u> all day and at night to be <u>eaten</u> … if this be pleasure, there is no doubt that I have been in Elysium for the last three weeks. But it

---

[2] William Watson (1744 - c.1825), a fellow of the Royal Society, a mathematician, founder of a philosophical society in Bath and a friend of John's father, William Herschel.
[3] Charles Babbage (1791-1871) Polymath extraordinaire. Mathematician, founder of the Analytical Society with Herschel, Peacock and others, elected a fellow of the Royal Society in 1816, co-founder of the Astronomical Society in 1820.

is worth taking some pains and undergoing some hardships to have seen this curious and most interesting country. I wish I had had more time at my disposal.

Snatches of entries from his personal journal – as well as the letters - are equally readable. One, dated June 27 said:

9:15 Reached the inn at Girgenti. Slept till 12 ½. Then moved a little, all asleep in the town & quite still. Town mean & Buggy. Inn tolerable (ie: not intolerable) 1:40 – Therm 76.1 fair in the shade … many ruins of old vaults hollowed inthe rock. Bought some antiques … . The homes have no glass windows … the shops (especially of eating & drinking) filthy … .

Neither Herschel nor the multitude of other English visitors who followed stinted on the negatives in their letters back home. Guide books were full of moaning as well. Bumpy carriages, slow trains, squalor, poverty and ignorance all hit travellers squarely between the eyes.[4] They didn't like haggling. Nor beggars. Nor the back-street whiff of decomposing refuse. Or the hostility to their Protestant beliefs. But invariably, all that was swiftly mitigated by the impact of the landscape, the frisson of antiquity, the good weather, the uncorsetted enjoyment of life. Grudges and grumbles soon evaporated. Much of Herschel's three days spent there were taken up with the usual sort of activities of 19th century British voyagers. Not only visiting the Greek temples, but also pursuing a compulsion for measuring the girths of surviving columns. Presenting letters of introduction to the local intelligentsia. Monitoring the rise in the broiling summer temperatures at regular intervals. Recording down to the last minute travelling times between his inn and the sights he was visiting. Dashing off correspondence to home and sketching whatever landscapes that caught his fancy.

Alexander was no stranger to either warm climates or to occasional discomfort. These had been his experiences in the Far East and, later, in South Africa. So, his grandfather's words would not have dampened him in the slightest. Indeed they seemed a beckoning, as were the idyllic sketches of the Sicilian countryside left behind by Sir John. Affecting him with far more immediacy, however, was a chance encounter in England. At some point, presumably early on in 1920, he met a Sicilian gentleman three years younger than he in London. An ardent Anglophile, the man came from time to time for a brief change of scenery, away from yet another winter on his distant island and to practice his English. As a *hotelier* by profession, he wanted to keep up to date on English tastes and what

---

[4] Howling continued well into modern days. In the letters column of The Morning Post July 25,1922, one visitor to Sicily wailed: 'If the Italian State Railways desire large numbers of tourists to visit Girgenti – and it is well worth a visit – they should organise a decent service of trains between Syracuse and Girgenti and between Girgenti and Palermo. The quickest train takes 10 ½ hours to cover the 163 miles between Syracuse and Girgenti and this journey involves taking both luncheon and dinner with one, for at the miserable railroad buffets on the way there is hardly anything to be had. The 84 ½ miles from Girgenti to Palermo cannot be accomplished in much less than five hours, so that the maximum of times must be spent upon the praiseworthy resolves to see the marvellous Greek temples'.

## Chapter 8

travellers expected on their trips abroad. He liked to come to London for a whiff of northern culture, to pursue some business, stock up on prized English goods unavailable back at home. Passionate about football, he mastered the rules of the games sufficiently there in England to introduce it to his home town and indeed create its first team. Whatever brought this man to *Albione* this time, his path would cross with Alexander's. The two were extremely cultivated and quite clearly had shared tastes. Their interests coincided. It wasn't long before the kindly Sicilian did what came naturally: he urged Captain Alexander Hardcastle to come south to Sicily and pay a visit to his town. Girgenti.

If Hardcastle was at a crossroad in his life, at least he knew the very first direction to chose. It took him to Number 1 Lake Buildings, St. James's Park in central London. It was not far from Belgravia where his family had lived for so long. 'Lake Buildings' was the Passport Office. It was where you went when you wanted to get out. And Alexander wanted to do just that in early October 1920. The Passport Office obliged on October 25 by issuing him his 32-page blue document of release: HM Passport Number 279892. The itch to travel, to redirect his life seemingly also touched his younger brother Henry Robert after his anaemic, short-lived career in the Anglican Church. Between 1901 and 1913, Harry had wafted from curacy to curacy, never making much of an indentation: Henley, Selly Oak, Shirley, Edgbaston and, finally, Bordesby, before gravitating back to the family hearth and a life of inactivity. What better opportunity than to tag along with his brother? And so, Henry Robert turned to Lake Buildings. Four days after Christmas, on December 29, 1920, he too was issued a passport, Number 308690. The two men were now ready.

# –9–

Dull, unrelenting poverty had been a fact of life in Sicily for as long as anyone could remember. Not in the few enclaves of exaggerated wealth and grandeur, of course, such as salons, clubs and grand hotels of Palermo and Messina. There, the denizens lived in 'voluptuous immobility', as the author Giuseppe di Lampedusa so bitingly put it, passing their days in monotonous, repetitive assembly and haemorrhaging money at the gaming tables. But for most others elsewhere, it was a different matter. Compounding the misery of their personal daily lives were the earthquakes and the volcanic eruptions of Etna which periodically dealt low blows: six sizeable quakes or eruptions had visited Sicily between the mid-1550s and 1928, including the devastating one at Messina in 1908. And economically, nowhere was the situation starker than at Girgenti. That province held the sorriest record of all: for years, it had the lowest per capita income of *all* among the provinces of Italy.

To be sure, some hives of hope and activity did buzz on the island as a whole. The Marsala wine trade, producing the sweet dessert elixir so loved on the tables of Europe and America, enjoyed great popularity ever since the early 1800s, giving work to many. Sulphur mining, with its many pros and cons, was in full swing. Shipping enjoyed a boom. In the first half of the 1800s, the island's commerce with England was ten times as great as with all the other Italian states put together. Archaeology, too, gave an injection of life to the island. With the encouragement of the British consul in Palermo, Robert Fagan, the Englishmen William Harris and Samuel Angell, both of them architects by training, began a two-year dig, between 1822-1823, at Selinunte, 62 miles along the southern coast, to the west of Girgenti. They brought to light three metopes – sculpted panels sited between triglyphs in a Doric frieze – dating from the early part of the 6$^{th}$ century BC. Sadly, Harris, scarcely 27 years old, died of malaria before he could leave the island. The discovery of these relics, of course, sparked even more curiosity among foreigners to come visit the ancient sites of Sicily.

Determined travellers were trickling in, bravely defying brigands, kidnappers, malaria and cholera, in order to see the relics of the past. In coping with one of the minor 'irritations' of travel, they were counselled that 'patience is the only armour against the importunity of the begging children.' Tourism was familiarly called 'l'industria dei forestieri'. Visitors politely closed their eyes to the fact that scarcely 250 miles of the island boasted carriage-able roads. For travel elsewhere in Sicily, it meant enduring gruelling muleback rides across the shadeless terrain, just as Alexander's grandfather had done or otherwise travel by boat. Mercifully, things began to change in that respect in

1863, when the very first leg of the island's railroad was inaugurated. It was only marginally faster than muleback transport, but at least it assured a greater degree of comfort. When it came, perhaps most vital to the welfare of southern Sicily, though, was the rail link from Palermo to Porto Empedocle which opened in 1876, running through Caltanissetta. This not only eased travel but also relieved some of the transport traffic of the all-important sulphur from the mines of central and southern Sicily to waiting ships at that port just south of Girgenti. Sulphur, that stuff that spewed over the landscape was like a 'yellow cloud of resentment', as one Victorian writer put it. Improved means of movement and marginally better lodgings brought in yet more. The grande dame of American letters, Edith Wharton, swooped in with her husband aboard a chartered yacht for her pilgrimage to the temples in 1888. The Anglo-American painter John Singer Sargent arrived later and painted several lovely watercolours.

George Dennis, the white-bearded writer-historian-diplomat, distinguished for his classic books, 'The Cities and Cemeteries of Etruria' and 'A Handbook for Travellers in Sicily', for whom Alexander would later develop the greatest esteem, took up the reins as British consul in Palermo in 1870 – two years before Hardcastle's birth.[1] Like his diplomatic colleagues elsewhere on the island, Dennis watched over all on his patch, reporting back to London: commercial activities, brigandage, disease epidemics. And about sulphur, too, that yellow gold which endemically short-changed the wretched miners, the *zolfatari,* who toiled long, thankless hours in boiling conditions below ground. They were forever at the mercy of the whims of the market and under the cloud of chronic unrest around them. If they were paid at all, it was a pittance that see-sawed between little and even less. *Carusi* – boys – as young as ten were dispatched into the mines, flouting unenforceable minimum-age labour laws. It was all in order to add to the family coffers, to pay for the ever rising cost of food. If the well-to-do gorged on *cannoli* and *cassata* at Christmas, 'holidays' for the poor meant some extra chickpeas or a handful of walnuts and almonds at the family table. If there was even a table.

In the province of Girgenti, in 1894, 18,400 men held down jobs of one sort or another. Of those, just over 11,000 were connected in some manner to the sulphur trade. This, out of an overall 27,000 sulphur miners throughout Sicily, working in a little under 300 operative mines. Norma Lorimer, the Scottish authoress, travelling through Girgenti in 1901 described the double-edged sword:

---

[1] Dennis made his very first visit to Sicily in 1847. It was on a later foray, in March 1863, seven years before his consular appointment to Palermo, that he brazenly began his own excavations at Capo Soprano near Gela. From accounts, it seems that he did not always trouble himself with the need of permissions. Archaeologist Paolo Orsi, in fact, recalled that Dennis was aided there by *'the characteristic figure'* of his wife, Nora, sitting on a field chair, protected from the sun *'by a large red parasol'*. Under her enormous bell-jar crinolines, she hid *'the most precious pieces which gradually came out of the tombs'*. Then, with the help of miserly bribes, the Dennises were able to spirit out about forty boxes containing 281 rare vases, terracotta figurines, lamps and other objects. Notwithstanding his sometimes uneven relations with the British Museum, many of his relics today stand on their display shelves.

> The wealth, and the poverty, and the horrible degradation of Girgenti are all the outcome of sulphur. The handsome corso, with its excellent shops and fine public buildings is the outcome of sulphur; so, too, are the filthy depravity and bestial types of the men and women living in the foul-smelling streets behind the corso … . No one is ashamed to beg in Girgenti … shouting at visitors 'Fame, signore, fame molta fame, piccola moneta'. I wonder if the sulphur kings of Sicily do anything for Girgenti … . [It is] a blister on the side of the island.

Clearly, she was an astute observer, particularly of the poor. The paupers of Girgenti subsisted on a daily ration of bread with perhaps a raw onion thrown in. These were citizens not on the way up the social ladder any time soon.

Mrs Neville Jackson, another early twentieth century traveller, focussed her curiosity even more on that accursed substance coming out of the earth, so vital in the production of gunpowder:

> the shafts are sunk deep and from dark passages come thin smoke and the dull booms of explosions which indicate blasting. Boys bear the yellow stuff … to the surface. When the ore is brought up it is melted in a calcarone or kiln, and the pure mineral [is] run off into moulds in which it cools and becomes the solid blocks we saw at the station. Each block weighs 122½ lbs., and when borne by mules one block is put on either side of the beast in hanging baskets or saddle-bags, two being a load. We met a long train of these asses in a country road near Girgenti, the port of Empedocles close by being one of the places where much of it is shipped. Enormous fortunes are made out of sulphur.

The sulphur kings, though, were living on counted days, about to be dethroned. They lived to the hilt while they could, buying cars and hiring chauffeurs to drive them ostentatiously around town. But those same cars were quietly to be hidden away in garages to collect dust as the money dwindled. As America improved its own ore extraction techniques and boasted a far purer variety, the price of sulphur fell dramatically. And with that, the Sicilian mining aristocracy was thrown into rapid turmoil and forced to close more and more mines. Riots at Porto Empedocle erupted; people were hungry; such food as was available was overpriced; jobs were starting to evaporate. In virtually all places surrounding Girgenti, massive strikes broke out. Sulphur miners vented their rage about their diminished fortunes. As if that weren't enough, fresh shoot-ups were a reminder that the Mafia was flexing its muscle. Not far away at Vittoria, near Ragusa, some of the first skirmishes between fascist sympathisers and communists had begun, bringing to the surface political as well as economic distress. More sparring ensued at Modica and neighbouring towns.

Girgenti had its own trigger-happy denizens, too, who wrote the ground rules for social conduct: men went out for evening strolls while it was frowned upon for ladies to do likewise. Womenfolk were expected to look down from the privacy of their latticed windows on to the *passeggiata*. Strollers were discouraged from looking back. And when

## Chapter 9

one man shot at the tolling church bells because of the noise they made, or another man pummelled a pedestrian for daring to wear clothing 'above his station in life', townsfolk looked on acceptingly and half-smiled.

*Cesare De Angelis studying Greek relics. (Courtesy of Gabriele De Angelis)*

It was into all of that very brittle landscape that Alick and Harry Hardcastle first stepped one brisk January day of 1921. The portly young patron of the newly-built

Belvedere Hotel in Girgenti who greeted the Hardcastle brothers that winter day in 1921 was Cesare De Angelis, or don Cesarino to his friends. Tall and graceful in an elephantine way, he walked with a delicate lope and displayed the very soft white hands of a gentleman. He had a handsome olive complexion, deep-set eyes and a pronounced nose. He combed his jet-black long wavy hair straight back and affected splendid white linen suits to complete the dashing overall effect. Until marriage, which came to him unusually late in life, De Angelis was very much the heart throb around town. When he finally did settle down, wedding one of the lady visitors to his hotel from northern Italy, his wife was, uncharitably, described by one patron as 'one of those yellow objects devastated by fever'. Don Cesarino's appearance, on the other hand, reminded English visitors to his hotel of a Sicilian Corney Grain, a large and jowly English entertainer and songwriter popular in the latter half of the 1800s. De Angelis hovered over his dining room tables eager to content the palates of his exigent outsiders. Lorimer remembered: 'Our gentle giant attends to our wants himself during meals. His manner is a subtle mixture of the dignity of a host and a humble anxiety for our comfort and his cooking is superb.' He had given his new premises several outdoor tiled terraces, all on different levels. Vine-covered pergolas had been added, to provide shade from the midday sun. From one of the terraces, you could look out to sea, while from another you peered down onto the Piazza Vittorio Emanuele. De Angelis arranged excursions for the increasing number of *'templari'*, or temple-goers, that came his way. He translated for them, showed off his private collection of antiquities, smoothed their way at every turn, always ready to carry out whatever favours were required. In short, he was the consummate *hotelier* and knew his trade well. The Belvedere had come down to him from his father, Oreste De Angelis who called the original place elsewhere in town the Belle Vue, *à la française*. All the well-honed skills were in the family of making outsiders feel welcome. He would smooth the way in the coming months for Alexander as well. In a letter back home recounting the activities of their early days, Harry wrote:

> On February 2, 1921 we went to Castel Vetrano and saw the ruins of Selinunte. Alick was much struck by the columns thrown down by earthquakes. On returning to Girgenti, Alick paid much attention to the Temple of Herackles which then consisted of seven columns prostrate, the drums apart showing daylight between them like the vertebrae of some monster.

It did not take long for Hardcastle to discover the enchantment of the place and to fall totally under its spell. In this, he was in good company. His respected compatriot Edward Hutton was to write in 'Cities of Sicily' that 'there can be few more wonderful sites left in the world than the spectacle which lies before one from the hills of Girgenti'. The utter beauty of the valley below, the mystery and the history of the temples, the wonderful climate and shimmering sea off in the distance all spelled magic. Alexander was bewitched. The two brothers stayed at the Belvedere for the coming months, clients of De Angelis. It gave them the time they needed to get their bearings in this town of some 20,000 souls, make new contacts and, most important of all, come to a vital decision: that of staying on at Girgenti and making it their home. Now all they needed was a place of their own. Once again, don Cesarino stepped in to help.

One thing was certain before long. They would *not* hunt for a base anywhere in the upper part of town, which had a grim, broken-down, fetid network of back streets just behind the elegant façade of the main boulevard, the via Atenea. Areas such as the Rabato, Bibirria and San Michele, where as many as ten luckless souls piled together into cramped quarters without running water, lighting or even a semblance of bathrooms. These were customers who only brushed with cleanliness for their wedding day or for the patron saint's day. Theirs were neighbourhoods so impoverished that even when they went to Sunday morning Mass, they took along their own chairs, to save on the cost of renting them … a practice adopted among equally hard-pressed churches. There were no friendly milkmen in those days either. A shepherd simply led his leashed animal from door to door. Housewives brought out jugs to be filled. No. It was all too dark, too insalubrious. For these two privacy-loving gentlemen, something more apart, further afield, was required. Who knows. Maybe something amidst the temples themselves?

The villa sat half way down the slope in the heart of the Valley of the Temples within the *contrada* of Civita. In the town property registry it had long been described as a 'countryside holiday home'. Long and narrowish, it stood two stories high. It was concealed from public view by compound walls eighteen feet high, all but sealing off the property. There was an imposing front gate giving access to the inside. Once through the entranceway, there was a good sized inner courtyard choked in vegetation and a railed ramp for vehicles leading directly up to the front door. The façade was vaguely gothicky. There were tapered Moorish windows ornamented with gargoyles and there was a crenelated edging to the roof. On the ground floor living quarters of the house, there were four spacious rooms, railroad-car fashion, one leading into the next. All of them featured windows with stunning views. Further lower ground rooms completed the villa. On the property were other outlying buildings, ideally suited for live-in staff. There was plenty of space to accommodate cars, to map out a proper Mediterranean garden, erect a chicken coop to keep poultry on the dining room table. *And* the land featured a honeycomb of tombs just off to one side, the better to remind any owner of the place's intimacy with Girgenti's ancient past.

The 19$^{th}$-century property had once belonged to one of the wealthiest families in town, the Gennuardis. Quite a number of glittering trinkets had been part of their personal portfolio. They had once owned sulphur mines, ships, vast properties and palaces. But the family had fallen on hard times when sulphur interests failed. The Gennuardis had thus had to divest various assets, including this villa. Over the years, the property had bobbed along on the parched landscape like an unloved terrestrial buoy, drifting from one ownership to the next. The proprietor in the spring of 1921 was Signora Serafina Schillaci, the widow of Luigi Montana. Neither maintenance nor improvements had been carried out very actively there and it was a depressing sight when don Cesarino took Alick and Harry Hardcastle down the hill from the hotel for a first look. There was a thick tangle of weeds and undergrowth discouraging their passage. No formal plantings had been done. None of the previous owners had pressed for a link-up with the town water system, opting instead for the precarious alternative of a makeshift tank to collect the sparse dribbles from a small nearby spring and from rainwater, whenever *that* fell. This was supplemented by whatever else that was brought in by donkeyback. The place was dusty and dirty and unloved. The interiors were worn and drab. The Montanas, in short, had used this bare-boned place as a simple no-frills summer place.

But then the two house-hunters leaned out the windows to inspect the landscape. They were speechless by what they saw. Laid out on an east-west axis, this open space offered grandstand views to their left of the Temple of Concord and to their right, of one single column still standing upright of the mighty remains of the Temple of Herakles. Here and there were eucalyptus trees, their silvery leaves giving off a fumed aroma into the air. And straight ahead, beyond the remains of the so-called Tomb of Theron and further on, the Temple of Æsculapius, lay the Mediterranean, glimmering in the sun. They had found their home. With no hesitation, they booked an appointment with a local notary Pietro Caverna, for May 2. The price tag in the neighbourhood of 3000 Lire made it a give-away for Alexander. On that date, the house became theirs. They would henceforth call the place the Villa Aurea, after the name of the nearby fourth – and most important – of the seven gateways into ancient Akragras, the Porta Aurea.

'All that first summer [Alick] was busy repairing the casino to live in', Harry wrote to the family back in England. When the Villa Aurea was at last liveable, the time had come to decamp from the Hotel Belvedere. The two brothers settled affairs with their affable hotelier. Almost as an afterthought, they gently observed that he perhaps might consider installing a further bathroom for the convenience of his customers, to supplement the only other one in the entire establishment. De Angelis quipped lightly that he didn't think he could afford it. With that, Alexander quietly summoned plumbers to outfit a new one on the ground floor, tucked discretely down the corridor leading to the area behind the front reception desk. He affixed a small plaque that read 'Dono di un amico inglese'. Gift of an English friend.

# –10–

'Lover of splendour, fairest of mortal cities, home of Persephone, thou that inhabitest the hill of noble dwellings, above the banks where feed sheep beside the stream of Akragas', wrote Pindar the great Greek lyric poet of the 5th century BC, in his twelfth Pythian Ode marking the triumph of Midas in a flute competition. Indeed ancient Akragas *was* reckoned by many to be fairest of mortal cities, a monument to wealth and magnificence and culture. It was a city whose name[1] and fortunes would change over the centuries.

Traditionally said to be founded in 580 BC by colonists from the coastal city of Gela, 37 miles to the east, and enlarged by a successive wave of fellow Greek settlers from Rhodes, the choice of location was shrewd, for Akragas was ideal in many respects. The site was strategically situated, roughly half way between Gela and Selinus (today's Selinunte), other important settlements. Thanks to a steep rock formation on the northern slope of the valley, the place would enjoy a measure of natural protection. Its port was at today's San Leone; as yet, however, excavations have not told us much about its size. Nonetheless, it was suitably placed to trade with the Carthaginians just across the water in North Africa and to keep a watchful eye on them.[2]

The terrain was fertile and its crops would go a long way towards ensuring great wealth to the area. Images on many of the minted coins bore witness to the idyllic wildlife that also flourished there: eagles, poppies, cicadas, butterflies. From the rich soil came prized olives sold on to north Africa; wheat which was dispatched to Athens; vineyards that turned out wines for yet others. Between the spoils that came with vanquishing the Carthaginians and the annexing of Himera on the northern coast, as well as the blessing of its own natural resources, the city's swelling coffers gave rise to a rich commercial class. It is popularly thought that it took its early name from one of the two nearby streams, the Akragas (today's Torrente San Biagio) which demarcated the eastern perimeter. Just how large the city came to be is not certain: the estimates did not always include slaves and children. Nevertheless, Akragas at its acme was reckoned to have perhaps 200,000 inhabitants, plus or minus serfs and the young. It was second only

---

[1] Agrigentum, with the Roman conquest. The Arabs renamed it, alternatively, Kerkent or Kerketi under their watch starting in 828. It was also called Gergent, then Grigentum and later Girgenti. On April 30, 1927, the Prefect informed citizens that 'the name of the town Girgenti is henceforth to be called Agrigento, effective with the new financial year beginning July 1, 1927'.

[2] A proper harbour, with jetties, was constructed between 1749-1763, using pillaged remains from the Temple of Zeus Olympios.

to Syracuse on the eastern side of Sicily. In short, it was a leading city of the Greek world.

Phalaris, the first tyrant, or ruler, between 570 and 555 BC gave Akragas its early outlines by building settlement ramparts. But it was under the more benevolent reign of Theron (488 - 472 BC) and later to a lesser degree of his son, Thrasydaeus, that the city truly prospered. Theron erected his own eight miles of defensive city walls to enclose the expanded city. They were of simple design with no complicated towers or bastions. They followed the natural contours of the land, running on top of ridges and folding in all rock formations en route. (Work to them by successive rulers continued over time) There were nine city gates giving access into the urban area. Because of the slope in the terrain, Akragas was set out on five tiers. At its pinnacle, 1000 feet high, is a ridge delineating the northern part of Akragas, split into two distinct camel-like humps, with a dip in between. The nearer of these two hills to the Valley is the Rock of Athena, or Rupe Atenea; the farther now constitutes modern-day Agrigento. The former was the site of the acropolis, where the sacred shrines and a military garrison stood. Clinging to the slope just below were the private homes and villas and shops. There were an upper and a lower agora, where the public assembled and the popular assembly gathered to appoint judges and to deliberate on those draft laws submitted by the council. In the area of the upper agora there were also the *bouleuterion*[3] and the *ekklesiasterion*[4].

Much of the architecture was a clear reflection of the city's great wealth and stature. The native philosopher Empedocles, who dressed in purple robes, or *chlamys*, donned golden sandals and gave himself a crown of laurel leaves, famously commented that 'they ate as though it were their last meal and built as if there were no tomorrow'. And on what an ostentatious scale was their lifestyle! These were not people who thought small. Exænetus, victorious in the foot race at the Olympic games, for example, was escorted back into Akragas with a procession of 300 chariots, each drawn by a pair of white horses. Another citizen, Antisthenes also believed that money was no object: for his daughter's marriage, he 'chauffeured' his guests to the event in some 800 chariots, while another well-to-do citizen, Gellias, prodigious in his hospitality, thought nothing of putting up 500 for the night. Yet another native boasted a 42-room villa there. And when pet birds died, it was not uncommon to give the creatures grand burials, graced with tombstones marking the spot. Wine cellars of the privileged were known to hold up to 30,000 amphoræ If one's personal flamboyance was truly on the grand scale, so too was the splendour of the public buildings and temples that went up as the city grew richer and richer.

It was along the southernmost wall, through Gate IV, the so-called Porta Aurea, that stood the most eye-catching plums of all. They were a magnificent row of temples that all went up during a surprisingly short but golden era of construction lasting scarcely ninety

---

[3] The externally quadrangular meeting place of the council chosen to draft laws for submission to the ecclesia, or popular assembly of citizens for final approval.

[4] Where the popular assembly gathered to appoint judges and to deliberate on those draft laws submitted by the council.

years. That glorious period ran from the very late 6<sup>th</sup> century BC through much of the 5<sup>th</sup>. On this east-west axis stood five of them, as well as a major sanctuary site containing further temples, shrines and altars. What may be the oldest temple to emerge from that period and believed, on the basis of Cicero's writings, to be in tribute to Herakles was built in the early Doric style in warm yellow tufa. It was in the peripteral form, meaning that it featured detached rows of columns wrapping around the cella, or enclosed inner sanctuary of the temple. The outer colonnade measured 239 feet in length and 89 feet in width. The two long sides had rows of 15 handsome columns each, surmounted by Doric capitals. It was this temple that was Alexander's closest 'neighbour'. It was this one, too, for which he embarked on perhaps his boldest enterprise throughout the years in southern Sicily.

*The Temple of Concord today with an outer row of thirteen columns. (Photo: the author)*

His other neighbour, to the east, was the so-called Temple of Concord. Of all the surviving monuments, this was the best preserved. Much written about by diarists, much etched by romantic artists, much photographed. It derived its name from the fragment of a 1<sup>st</sup>c. AD tablet found nearby, inscribed in Latin, partially reading *Concordiae Agrigentinorum*. The 'concord' part has stuck ever since. It had many features in common with the Temple of Herakles. It is also of peripteral form, as temples there usually were by this stage; there is an outer row with 13 columns running the full 138-foot length of the structure and another two rows, each counting six columns, at both ends of the temple. During the Middle Ages, it was used as a church, which accounts for its good state of preservation. It also accounts for the architectural changes within where arched openings along the sides of the cella, the enclosed inner room, were introduced. No less important were the remains of the so-called Temple of Hera Lakinia (Juno Lacinia) at the southeast corner of the city walls, the Zeus Olympios or the Olympieion (Jupiter) just to the north of the Porta Aurea and beyond that, the Temples of the Dioscuri (Castor and Pollux) and Hephaistos (Vulcan).

The glory of Akragas came to an end in 406 BC when the Carthaginians besieged and took the city, evicting most of its inhabitants who sought calmer waters elsewhere. Although they were later allowed to return, the city's enclosures by then were badly pummelled. Akragas slowly recovered until the outbreak of the first Punic war (264-241 BC) between Rome and Carthage. Although these two great powers drifted almost accidentally into hostilities, it was probably inevitable that a clash of interests would develop between the Mediterranean's foremost sea power and an expanding Rome that by the third century BC controlled southern Italy. Sicily became the battleground and Akragas, so close to Carthage across the water, was sacked or burned three times between 261 and 211 BC. With Rome's victory came a long period of peace and a change of name, to Agrigentum.

Relatively little is known of Agrigentum during those long years of tranquillity under the mantle of Rome, but archaeological evidence suggests a modest prosperity. Now that the Sicilian countryside was safe along with its corn, wine and livestock so essential to Rome and other of its dominions, the pattern of settlement changed. The population of the countryside grew and the old Greek fortified wall-town declined in importance or was simply abandoned. Coastal towns like Agrigentum fared better, but it is not thought to have had more than 16,000 inhabitants under the early Empire. Sicily's other main cities did little better. These years saw, however, the early development of sulphur mines around Agrigentum, which undoubtedly brought some revenue to the city, as did its export of bitumen, much valued for the caulking of ships. The general picture remains, however, of a modest provincial backwater.

Peace, sadly, would not last forever. From about AD 440, the Vandals began their invasions of Sicily and strife was renewed. Like a chess pawn, the island changed hands, passing from the Vandals back to Rome, then became a Byzantine province ruled from Constantinople. In AD 828 it fell again, this time to the Arabs, whereupon it changed name once again, becoming Kerkent or Kerketi. For nearly 260 years the Arabs imparted large chunks of their language, architecture and culture to Sicily, Kerkent included. But that, too, did not last indefinitely. Once again, in 1086, the town was taken, this time by the Normans invading from the mainland. King Roger I founded a well-endowed bishopric and the name of Girgenti was adopted.

But over the centuries, it was *ancient* Akragas and her antiquities that had brought outsiders to visit: not only writers who penned enticing accounts of their travels here, but also historians who undertook serious studies and recorded their findings about the city's early history. Father Giuseppe Maria Pancrazi, a Tuscan, for example, arrived for the first time in 1728 and devoted many years to the island, eager to redress the relative paucity of

## Chapter 10

writings about Sicilian antiquities. In 1751, the first edition of his book 'Antichità Siciliane spiegate' was published in Naples. The Amsterdam-born J. Philippe D'Orville came in about the same period. Julius Schübring from Germany followed in the next century. Robert Koldewey and Otto Puchstein weighed in as well with a respected co-authored book published in 1899, 'Die griechischen Tempel in Unteritalien und Sicilien'. On canvas, artists such as Phillip Hackert and Jean Houel did much to romanticise and to immortalise the ruins, too. Formal excavations and restorations, of course, ensued, following hand-in-hand with the increased recognition of the importance of these sites. A leading light throughout the 1830s was Domenico Lo Faso Pietrasanta, Duke of Serradifalco who headed the newborn Commission for Antiquities and Fine Arts. Under his directorship, many excavations and restorations went forward, including ones in Girgenti at the Temples of Demeter and of Herakles and at the Temple of the Dioscuri (Castor and Pollux), where four columns were resurrected 'picturesquely' if not with 'scientific rigour', a patchwork pastiche of hijacked pieces from other neighbouring buildings. As the American writer Henry James Forman summed it up lightly, 'Sicily is the archaeologist's picnic ground.' Indeed it was. And Alexander Hardcastle stood poised there in Girgenti in the early days of 1921, basket in hand, ready for the feast.

# -11-

Peering out the windows of the Villa Aurea, Hardcastle could see a rippling carpet of white before him. It was that of early spring blooms on the perfumed almond trees, covering the slopes as far as the eye could see. His compatriot, Mrs Jackson, likened this vision to 'a mist', while another, Mrs Alec (Ethel Brilliana) Tweedie, described the sight of thousands of almond trees 'like a field of snow in March'. Yet a third gushed that 'we strove knee-deep through flowers into the Temple … '. Once he had signed the deed of purchase to the Villa, however, Alexander had a far more pressing agenda than simply to gaze out at almond blossoms.

*Present-day view of the Villa Aurea terrace, much as Hardcastle left it. (Photo: the author)*

## Chapter 11

This was a large house – the very first one he had ever owned himself – to get into habitable shape. When he finished installing new bathrooms and grafting a proper kitchen onto the eastern side of the villa, he then added a triangular terrace some 82 feet long, that took in an almost full sweep of the temples. The terrace was surfaced with a dizzying jigsaw of brightly patterned Sicilian tiles: there were swirling pale blue and white ones side by side with others squiggly black and grey and elsewhere, squares of chocolate brown. All were mixed in jumbled excitement. The dozen or so rooms in the main house had to be furnished. Sturdy new cisterns were installed to store the meagre water supplies gurgling up from the property's small spring and from the fitful drizzle of rainfall. These sources would make do until such time as he could be hooked up to a more assured supply from the town's mains. During dire shortages, he would resort as most others did, to jugs brought in on donkey back. The house adjacent to his would accommodate his staff and that staff, too, had to be engaged. Gaetano Marchica, in due course, would enter his service as faithful retainer, while Marchica's wife reigned in the kitchen. Off to the other side of the compound, Alexander added garaging for cars.

Furnishings appeared and the place gradually took on a semblance of domesticity. A beautiful gold table clock appeared in the parlour, while a carved chest went into the hallway in which to store the brothers' record collection. The gramophone went into one of the front rooms. Deck chairs were bought for the terrace, as were some potted succulents, *alla siciliana*. A few squat palms, too, helped fill out the terrace greenery, planted in raised brick-edged flower beds. They still survive today. Alick and Harry could be seen along the smart Via Atenea in early summer lugging supplies and furnishings themselves back to their retreat rather than entrusting them to shopkeepers for delivery. That very sight, of two foreign *gentiluomini* sullying their hands with the humble tasks of the underclass, entered local lore! Particularly since the street was normally given over to much elegant posturing among the élite. This was an era when it was even considered poor form in the bourgeoisie for a man to leave home hatless. And thus, nearly one century later, the tale is still told about the two Englishmen who actually carried their own purchases through town.

As in many Italian homes, the floors were tiled, the better to keep the interiors cool. They chose a diamond-shaped pattern, somewhat gothicky, in keeping with the tastes of the times. The two bachelors gave little thought to the walls: a plain-framed mirror here, a photograph there, a replica of Leonardo da Vinci's 'Gioconda' and a mounted document elsewhere. Sculpted busts of classical luminaries, however, made their way into the parlour and onto the terrace later on.

Records do not survive indicating how many belongings the two men brought with them from England, how many were sent for subsequently and how many were simply acquired locally. As of their departure date from England in early 1921, neither parent had yet died. It is a fair guess that no family memorabilia was in their luggage. But one item for certain was in Alexander's possession there: a small telescope, most likely crafted by one of his Herschel ancestors. Over the following years, the Girgentini would remember him raptly fixed on the heavens after dark, looking through his telescope.

*Sitting room of the Villa Aurea, 1920s.*

Alexander did not waste time in other respects. He was anxious, it is true, to get his new house up and running as quickly as possible. But, equally, he was restless to take on something far more ambitious. Harry recalled the regular mantra around the new household regarding the nearby Temple of Herakles: 'He would say repeatedly that some one should put up the columns. As soon as the house was finished, he took the thing in hand.'

Erected at the end of the sixth century BC, it was reckoned to be even more imposing than the later Temple of Concord nearby. It was 221 feet long, based on the dimensions of the stylobate, and its pillars rose higher – by 11 feet – than those of Concord. There was something of the David-and-Goliath about this challenge. After all, he was still something of an unknown quantity there in rural Sicily. He and his brother were the sole foreigners at that time living in Girgenti. No one quite knew why he had come. Was he a crank of some sort? Would it be rash to place faith in an outsider? He had scarcely a handful of new friends there. He did not yet speak the language of his newly-adopted home. The challenge he set for himself was to help jump-start restorations and excavations in the Valley of the Temples where such work only spluttered along when funding permitted.

To that end, he sat down at his desk in late May 1921, barely weeks after purchasing the Villa and drafted a letter for Rome. He enlisted De Angelis to translate it into Italian. It was addressed to the Central Department of Fine Arts (Direzione Generale delle Belle Arti) within the Ministry of Education.[1] They held the puppet strings to make things happen, as well as the sometime threadbare purse strings to pay the way. Would the esteemed high authorities of the Ministry consider his proposal to part-finance the raising of three or four of the 33-foot high columns of the Temple of Herakles there in the Valley? The crumbled heap of fluted stone lay on the south side of the temple and Alexander, with his engineering background, saw no excessive difficulty in getting them upright again. For this, he wrote, he stood ready to contribute 20,000 Lire. In 1921, daily labourers in Girgenti were fetching 11 Lire for one day's work. Alexander's offer was thus the equivalent of putting twenty men on payroll for a full three months. This was also a period when the entire budget for archaeological work and maintenance *in Italy* stood at 39 million Lire, while New York's Metropolitan Museum of Art *alone* disbursed $1.1 million. With the dollar-lire rate of exchange then in force, it meant that Italy's earmarked funding for the entire country scarcely exceeded, by $500,000, the Metropolitan's budget. Rome rarely received such letters from strangers. This was not one to be lost in the shuffle. They deliberated for several days, one imagines in a state of stunned disbelief.

Nudging things along from the sidelines was Filippo Mendolìa who had twice served as mayor of Girgenti and was currently the spokesman for local antiquities. Mendolìa clearly saw what the restorations might promise for his city. A fresh new spotlight on the Valley of the Temples and a greater influx of visitors, for starters. Rome then conferred with an expert from the Department of Archaeological Excavations and Museums in Palermo, Francesco Valenti, later to become a Superintendent of Monuments in Sicily, as to the feasibility of the undertaking. When he enthused, the reply came through to Girgenti. On June 4, they wrote that they would indeed take the Englishman up on his offer. What was more, they would evenly match his sum. Alexander was on his way. Sort of.

Late June, meanwhile, saw some new faces in Rome: Giovanni Giolitti was out as prime minister and Ivanoe Bonomi came in. Shortly afterwards, there was a cataclysmic loss for the opera world: the great tenor Enrico Caruso was dead and 50,000 people poured out onto the streets of Naples on August 5th, to pay their last respects. The breast-beating emotions of Naples, though, passed Hardcastle by. Alexander was instead in the throes of some personal matters: he wrote to the British Consulate in Palermo requesting

---

[1] At the time, it was this ministry that oversaw all archaeological sites in Italy.

a good conduct certificate. He needed it, he explained, in order to purchase a sporting gun and a revolver for his free moments, to go hunting in the hills around Girgenti. Migratory birds flying over Sicily drew the gun barrels of many local hunters and Hardcastle wanted to be one of them. It was further evidence that he was settling in![2]

In Girgenti, with exquisite slowness, the snail-paced red tape was set into motion and a skilled engineer appointed to orchestrate the upcoming work at the Temple of Herakles. A succession of 'experts' shuttled back and forth from Palermo. It seemed endless to Alexander's foreign eyes and it meant, unfortunately, that the work itself was still months away from starting.

Nonetheless, Hardcastle's magnanimous gesture had already catapulted him into the local limelight. It sent a signal of earnest renewed interest in the valley. When Prince Umberto of Savoy, heir to the Italian throne, sailed into nearby Porto Empedocle aboard the royal yacht on September 11, 1921, Girgenti shifted into high gear for its royal visitor. All the local dignitaries assembled, farcically elbowing one another at the wharf, jockeying for a ringside glimpse of the arrival, perhaps hoping for a handshake, a nod or even a word or two with the prince. The prefect Giovanni Garzaroli gluttonously guarded the lion share of the spotlight all for himself and ordered an arm-bearing cordon of policemen to keep viewers at a distance from their future sovereign. Those excluded even included the acting mayor of Girgenti, Michele Gaglio, who was not amused by the affront. Just about the only notable not down at the port at 8:00 a.m. that morning for the mooring was the solitude-loving Englishman.

Alexander had no appetite for a portside melée. He did not need to engage in an undignified push and shove. The show was coming to him. High on the royal agenda that morning, in fact, was a visit to the Valley. And that meant a stopover, without all the elbowing, at the Temple of Herakles with its new benefactor, its new champion. Valenti had already briefed the prince and Umberto was curious to meet the Englishman. Unlike most in his local entourage, the prince spoke English and was able to chat amiably about the restorations soon to take place. The meeting between the two thrust Hardcastle even more on centre stage. Suddenly, he was becoming an important star in the Girgenti galaxy.

Less than two months later, the spectre of fascism inched forward another step: on November 7, Benito Mussolini proclaimed himself 'Il Duce'. He, too, was increasingly on the map, in far off Rome. His politics were also making inroads in Sicily in some provinces, making empty promises of jobs for the labour-hungry islanders. Girgenti did not bite at the unbaited fish hook.

An article in The Illustrated London News of April 22, 1922 reported: 'In

---

[2] He turned to his consulate for other favours over the coming years: a good-conduct certificate for his brother Harry, so that he, too, could go hunting; further certificates required for car purchase; help in pursuing a petty thief who had pick pocketed the naïve Henry in the Palermo railroad station. Most significantly, he was to seek advice in late November 1924 on how to make an Italian will.

*Chapter 11*

accordance with the agreement made last year between the Italian Government and Captain Hardcastle, the restoration of this fine old Doric temple of Hercules of the 6th century BC will now be commenced and the raising of the ... best-preserved columns should be complete by this summer.'

The thud of wooden planks being stacked nearby in preparation for work was soon heard, as materials started to amass. Then came the incessant bang of carpenters' nails, as the Girgenti workforce slowly erected scaffolding around each column base. Ladders were perched against the platforms, to access the upper reaches of these Heath-Robinson-like structures. The massive four drums of each column were then hoisted up on pulleys, one by one, to the required height and swung over to be slotted into place, taking care to align the fluting in a single upward flow. Working with such primitive equipment, there were risks and indeed, one labourer was killed. Alexander immediately, quietly, came forth to cover both the funeral expenses and reparations to the widow.

*Scaffolding erected during restoration of the columns of the Temple of Herackles, Girgenti in 1923.*
*(From Karl Gröber, Sicilia, Augsburg, 1924)*

In all, there were seven columns to be resurrected, added to the one column that had survived intact throughout history. Confusingly, contemporary accounts talk of a 'four plus four' operation that took place in the 1920s. Given that the initial outlay of funds amounted to 40,000 Lire, while the second allotment of money for the remaining columns came to 60,000 Lire, it might be reasonable to assume that the initial project, costing less, involved a fewer number of columns, while the more expensive project that followed covered a larger number of columns. Thus it would have been a 'three plus four' project. On the other hand, in an account that Harry left behind after Alexander's death, he, too, refers to 'four plus four'. Perhaps the one upright column teetered perilously and needed further reinforcement and restorations and thus the work got counted as an extra column. Whichever the case, 1922 was a very busy year for Alexander.

The political tectonics of Italy during this time were scraping angrily. Fascist thuggery under the aegis of Mussolini's *squadristi,* or bullyboys, was metastasicing throughout the country. Insurrections were staged in Fiume, Bologna, Milan. Opposition newspapers were being systematically destroyed. Governments were short-lived. Political tensions in Girgenti were not yet in high gear nor had they yet touched the two brothers directly. On September 16, 1922, a full 20 months after their arrival, the local prefecture finally got around to reporting their presence to the Public Security Department of the Ministry of the Interior in Rome, as was mandatory. Alas, they could not spell the surname correctly (Hardcastel), nor record their ages accurately. The prefecture was equally approximate in stating when they had actually arrived, typing in 'da vario tempo' or some time ago. They had been around long enough, though, for the authorities to now restyle them as 'Alessandro' and 'Enrico' on official documents!

Alick all this while was evermore focussed on the insular world of archaeology and his very own moves. He yearned to see the Herakles project completed, the final columns rise once more. Once again, he approached the authorities in Rome and specifically Arduino Colasanti who headed the clearing house for such projects, to offer a sum to move forward. This time, however, Rome's coffers were dry. There was no hope for help from the Ministry of Education. Nonetheless, they wrote back to Alexander. Yes, they replied, indeed the remaining columns *could* go up, but with no assistance from them. Not daunted, the Englishman agreed to single-handedly advance the 60,000 Lire needed to complete the job. He wanted to see all eight yellow tufa columns upright, in elegant alignment. For himself to see, for the world to enjoy.

In the meantime, across the Mediterranean Sea, the frenzy of excitement had just begun in earnest for another archaeological wonder: the discovery of Tutankhamen's burial site in early November by Howard Carter in Egypt's Valley of the Kings. That event was emblazoned across all the newspapers and magazines in England. The reading public could not get enough of these exciting new finds and the press was happy to oblige with more and more accounts.

Activities in Sicily seemed, somehow, to overshadow developments brewing very much on the personal front. Alick and Harry's father, Henry, was fading fast at Moor

## Chapter 11

House, outside Oxted. He was now 81 years old. Drink had been a faithful companion in his later years and he had had his share of disappointments over the years, with his eldest son tragically dead to tuberculosis and Alexander a victim of mental illness. His vast brood of children had spread their wings and left him in quiet decline, with Maria Sophia at his side. On March 10, 1922 The Times reported the inevitable sad news on Page 1: He had died at home the day before, Thursday March 9. The funeral service took place three days later at Oxted's St. Mary's Parish Church. Shortly after 2:30 that Monday afternoon, he was buried there in the church yard.

In due course, elaborate sculpted stone tombstones would be commissioned for him and his wife to mark the spot of their burials.[3] As was the custom then, after the death announcement, subsequent newspaper accounts of the funeral service gave detailed lists of the attendees from among the immediate family circle and whichever other notables were present. Nowhere in the articles that came out about Henry Hardcastle's funeral service in Oxted do the names Alexander and Henry Robert appear. They had not set foot outside Italy to pay their final respects to their father. Maybe this, too, was further conclusive proof of just how deep the family divide had been.

---

[3] Many of the tombstone inscriptions in the following decades weathered and have now faded to illegibility. The Church does not have any surviving records indicating the precise location of the Hardcastle burial plots.

# –12–

Alexander rapidly mastered a new sort of engineering skill: that of media engineering. He understood the importance of stimulating news coverage of Girgenti. It could help bear additional pressure on Rome, to accelerate work to be done in the Valley of the Temples. It would lead to the generation of jobs for the employment-hungry local labourers. It would draw ever more visitors to the classical sites and inject more money into the parched local economy. And hopefully, it would inspire more restorations in future years. Single-mindedly, he cultivated the press in England, doing all that he could to attract the spotlight onto 'his' corner of Sicily. But he knew that it would be more effective if the burden of promotion were shared. To this end he turned to Rome and enlisted the help of a fellow countryman two years his junior, the erudite, trim-bearded Dr. Thomas Ashby.

Ashby was a longstanding resident of Rome, a gentle-mannered Italophile who had spent his childhood with his Quaker family there. He was an architectural historian and a trained archaeologist. In 1906, he was appointed director of the then-named British School of Archaeology, History and Letters of Rome, a post he held for 15 years. He wrote prolifically, his chief focus being on classical Rome. His interests, however, were far broader, as were his connections with the British press. And he certainly was not averse to reporting developments *anywhere* throughout Italy, including advances being made in Sicily. He was drawn notably to the excavations at Motya Island, near the coastal town of Marsala. The land there had been acquired piecemeal by Joseph ('Pip') Whitaker of Marsala wine fame, expressly to uncover the rich trove of Phoenician relics that he knew to be there. The more that was discovered, the greater Whitaker's enthusiasm, helped and encouraged with the blessings of Antonino Salinas, director of the National Museum in Palermo.

It was perfectly natural that all Whitaker's activity should catch the eye of his fellow countryman, Ashby, and bring him south to see for himself. And it was equally logical for Ashby to have made contact with Hardcastle, lured by all that was also happening at Girgenti. Together, Ashby and Hardcastle could collaborate to bring Girgenti more into the international limelight. Being on the spot, Alexander could 'feed' Ashby photographs and information. Ashby would do the write-ups, as his name was well-known in England and opened doors readily. Specialist journals such as *Antiquity*, which started up in 1927, were an obvious outlet, of course. But Alick shrewdly saw greater advantage to write-ups in the popular press: the audience was far wider. It would be these readers, lots of them, who were tomorrow's southbound travellers. The Times and The Illustrated London

*Chapter 12*

News became faithful takers, sympathetic to the topic of new discoveries. Ashby was happy to oblige. Every time something appeared in print, Hardcastle was quick to send off copies to the people who counted in his circle. It went a long way to reinforce his own influence and give him leverage at the Ministry in Rome.

The people of Alexander's inner sanctum, those who mattered and whose fraternity and collaboration needed to be courted, were a small but important handful. With this coterie on his side, things were possible. Without them, he'd remain at a standstill. Besides, he was in tune with their tastes and their enthusiasms: they were the sort of intellectuals that he cherished. He reckoned that the crucial quartet to befriend consisted in, at the top, Roberto Paribeni in Rome, followed by Paolo Orsi in Syracuse. In Palermo and Girgenti, there were Pirro Marconi and Francesco Sinatra.

Paribeni was born in Rome in 1876 and thus four years younger than Alick. By his mid-twenties, his career seemed on the fast track. With a solid education in Rome behind him, followed by an apprenticeship with the Italian Archaeological School in Athens, Paribeni was then dispatched to digs in Crete. Returning home, aged thirty-two, he headed the Museo Nazionale Romano, in Rome and a further museum in Naples and took on the superintendency of antiquities for Rome and the Lazio region as well. Moving higher up the ladder, he then led archaeological missions to Turkey, Albania and Egypt, among other places.

*Roberto Paribeni*

Most important to Hardcastle, however, Paribeni was named Director General of Antiquities and Fine Arts for all of Italy in 1928, taking over the reins from Arduino Colasanti. Alexander certainly had been busy up until that date, but by the late 1920s he was fully in his stride. Remaining on friendly footing with Rome was all-important and the records show that a cordial rapport flourished, with many letters written between the two. Paribeni was to keep that post up to 1933, the year that Hardcastle died. Books and a professorship at Milan's Cattolica University added further lustre to his professional dossier. Despite all these heavyweight credentials and the imposing image of him with his thick-set neck, gold-rimmed spectacles and carefully trimmed, bib-shaped beard, Paribeni had an engagingly modest side to him as well. Once, observing some naked youths clambering among the rocks at an excavation site in Eritrea, he sat down, needle and thread in hand, and proceeded to clumsily stitch together clothing for them. Not the standard image of a well-born Italian male intellectual in the early 1920s!

But it was his role as Director General, during Hardcastle's Girgenti years, manning the 'traffic signals' in Italian archaeology, as it were, that mattered to the Englishman. It was Paribeni who determined when and when not to give the green light to excavations and to restorations throughout the country. It was he who allotted the required government funding, cleared appointments and promotions of archaeologists to specific projects and gave the go-ahead. Paribeni, in other words, had the final say. From time to time, Alick felt it opportune to take the overnight steamship from Palermo to Naples and then train it north to Rome. The odd visit to the top never hurt. Hardcastle may have had the money. But Paribeni had the say-so[1].

One rung lower on the ladder, but by no means less eminent, was Paolo Orsi at Syracuse, on the south-eastern shores of Sicily, by one called a '*Maestro principe dello scavo*' or princely master of excavations. In the early part of the 1920s, the superintendency there embraced a rather restricted parish. It only covered the two provinces of Catania and Syracuse. But after 1924, Syracuse was 'upgraded' to being superintendency for the antiquities of *all* Sicily and thus Orsi's responsibilities grew. He was conducting *his own* excavations as well as overseeing those of his colleagues elsewhere in Sicily. He was handpicking the teams to send out to all work sites on the island and ensuring that their work was properly done. He was writing up reports on all of them as well as articles for specialist journals. He was busy enriching the collections of his own museum in Syracuse, with a special emphasis on coinage for the numismatic department.

Orsi was a northerner, born at Rovereto, between Verona and Trento, in 1859. That made him, in the eyes of his Italian colleagues, virtually a German! Indeed, he *was* by birth a German national until he later took out Italian citizenship. He studied at Padua

---

[1] Five years after Hardcastle's death, Paribeni would blemish his own name and academic standing by being a signatory to the repugnant 'Manifesto of Racist Scientists', an open letter published on July 14, 1938 in the *Giornale d'Italia* which preceded the introduction of Mussolini's racial laws.

and Vienna, completing his degree in Rome. This was followed by studies at the Royal Italian School of Archaeology, also in Rome. After biding his time with early stints as a teacher in Lazio and an assistant librarian of the National Library in Florence, Orsi took the exams which won him entry into the archaeological world.

*Paolo Orsi*

His very first assignment was as inspector of excavations and museums and in that capacity, he was dispatched off to Syracuse in September 1888 as the second in command to Francesco Saverio Cavallari at the local Archaeological Museum. Orsi added Reggio Calabria, just across the Strait of Messina, to his dossier, taking up the reins as director of the newly-created Superintendency there. He then formally returned to Syracuse, full time, in 1924. Tall, thin and of ramrod military bearing, he wore his buttoned-up jackets and high laced boots much of the year, oblivious of broiling summer temperatures. This tenue was sometimes embellished with a swirling black cape. Throughout his long decades on the island, he called home his small ascetic hotel room, a stone's throw from his office. It counted one bed, two chairs and a single desk. Seemingly this Franciscan lifestyle suited the austere Orsi who eschewed anything of a social life. Every morning before daybreak, between 5:00-6:00 a.m., he'd shuffle the short distance from 'home' to the great door of the museum and unlock it himself to begin his day's labours. It was joked that Orsi was 'the very first person of the day to be outdoors in Syracuse ... even before the street sweepers'. More often than not, he and his office were operating on a budget about as threadbare as his hotel room. To save money, he frequently would forego his per diem when out on mission. He was made a senator in 1924 and as such, was entitled to first class train travel. But to keep within his narrow margins, he chose second class tickets for trips to Rome. The difference went back into the kitty. It may well have coloured his personal feelings towards Hardcastle who so easily could dip into his bank account, while he, Orsi, had the constant humiliation of having to plead with Rome for decent funding. However tinged his thoughts of envy or resentment might have been, he kept them successfully in check. His extravagances seemed to be restricted to a steady supply of cigars and an occasional sharp tongue. In one tail-stinging note to a colleague discussing the pecking order of works to be done, he addresses the question of on-site expenses. 'As inspector you are, of course, not entitled to claim for kilometres travelled; no one is reimbursed for rounds within the temple area. When you come and go [from the town above] you shall put in for the modest sum of a carriage ride. Whether you then decide to travel by carriage, in a hot-air balloon or on foot is of no concern to me.'

Orsi worked and wrote prodigiously; in his lifetime he produced well over 400 publications. While he was at home with virtually any historical era, it was the pre-Hellenic tribes of Sicily, the *Siculi,* in particular who captured his affections. It was Orsi's task to keep disciplinary tabs on the eager Englishman down the coast. Too much pillaging of antiquities had been going on. If he could not stem it altogether, at least he would slow down this sorry activity as much as possible. He committed Alexander to regular pledges to hold off his shovel. Quite reasonably, Hardcastle was not to ship off anything to the likes of the British Museum unreported and unauthorized.

The two men in their respective eyries were very similar. Both were northern-thinking do-ers with little patience for the *mañana* approach. They fired off letters to one another and received rapid replies. Neither had married. And both had wholly given over much of their adult lives to the passionate pursuit of archaeology in one of the richest hunting ground of them all. It little mattered that each focussed on different epochs of ancient history. The two men were on the same wavelength.

It was out on excavation missions that Orsi contracted malaria – a frequent risk in Sicily. Damp nights dossed down on camp beds exacerbated the arthritis in his limbs, while emphysema whittled away at his breathing. By his early 70s, Orsi was seriously weakened by this trio of afflictions and finally died, aged 76, in 1935.

Several years after Hardcastle's arrival at Girgenti, yet another northerner came on to the scene. He was young, brilliant, attractive and reckoned to be a most promising high flyer. Pirro Marconi was born in Verona in 1897 into a musical family. His father was first violinist with the Verona Opera Company orchestra, while his mother was a pianist. With the outbreak of The Great War, Pirro Marconi joined the Alpine Corps – an experience shared with Orsi – and saw constant action in the mountain peaks surrounding his homeland. During one particularly fierce battle, the 19-year old was wounded but refused to abandon his post, for which he was decorated at war's end. A lifelong love of his native mountains developed and he would return there for holidays whenever he could. He earned his first degree at Rome University in 1920. His thesis was devoted to the imagery of Antinous.[2]

*Pirro Marconi (Courtesy of the Butrint Foundation and the Museo Civiltà Romana)*

From Rome, Marconi then moved on to Athens in 1922, one of only four students accepted, to take courses at the School of Archaeology, as Paribeni had done. A further degree followed back in Rome in philosophy, and another in archaeology, conferred in September 1925. He then passed the exams for entry into the civil service and his very first brief assignment was as an assistant inspector of monuments in Padua. Orsi from Syracuse had his eye on this rising star and recommended his transfer to Sicily. At the outset, he was not on a fixed salary there, but was paid on a daily basis for each assignment put his way. Based in Palermo at the National Museum, Marconi eagerly began making forays south to Girgenti. It fell under his umbrella and proved a fertile place to show his mettle. Marconi was 25 years younger than Hardcastle. The age gap, however, did not deter the two from forming an intellectual bond. The more seamlessly they worked together, the less Marconi's financial concerns. The self-assured young Veronese, who regularly dressed in jodhpurs, high boots and sported a jaunty Canadian Mountie-styled hat against the sun, looked up to the Englishman and Hardcastle for his part instinctively trusted Marconi implicitly.

---

[2] On the premature death in AD130 of the handsome Antinous, Hadrian's young lover, the grieving Emperor commissioned a large number of sculptural and numismatic likenesses of him.

The remaining figure of the quartet was a local man, Sicilian to the core. His name was Francesco Sinatra. He lived up the hill from the Valley of the Temples on the fashionable tree-lined boulevard, the Viale della Vittoria. He was tall and meticulously trim and had a kindly face with high cheekbones. One of nine children, he pursued his studies at the University of Palermo and upon graduation there in 1898, aged 23, began teaching geography to gymnasium-level students back in Girgenti and, briefly, at nearby Sciacca. Income from the family haberdashery and fabric business on the Via Atenea had given Francesco Sinatra's brother Giuseppe the wherewithal to pursue a passionate new interest in art. In particular the luminous Impressionist-like Sicilian landscapes of Francesco Lojacono. Giuseppe, in a fifteen year period, would amass no less than 84 of the *maestro's* works. In the meantime, brother Francesco Sinatra kept up his geography lessons and, later, increasingly had to help manage the family business when it went through a difficult patch. On the side, he maintained a proprietary eye on the family lands nearby and then began gravitating more and more towards local civic responsibilities: from setting up a chamber of commerce to engaging performers for the local theatre, from joining the town council to running the tourist board. Sinatra loved horses and as a gesture of friendship, Alick gave him a white stallion on which to roam the hillsides. In 1925, Paolo Orsi came to town to appoint Sinatra to a newly-created post: Honorary Inspector of Monuments for Girgenti and its surroundings. It was the role that the cultivated Sinatra cherished most of all. And it was in that role that Alick had most in common with Francesco Sinatra.[3]

---

[3] A fifth person with whom all had to deal in that general period was the Naples-born Ettore Gabrici who was four years older than Hardcastle. After assignments in Naples, Florence and Rome, in 1914 he bid for the post of director of the Archaeological Museum in Palermo and was accepted. The thrust of his work there was initially on the excavations at Selinunte. Ancient coinage was his true passion and he wrote much on numismatics. With his promotion in 1926 to superintendent of archaeology in Palermo, his parish expanded to include Girgenti and Trapani. The steel-hearted Gabrici seemingly had a prickly personality and found it particularly difficult to get along with foreigners. Joseph 'Pip' Whitaker's explorations on Motya, for instance, were brought to a halt during World War I at the express instructions of Gabrici. Declared a site of 'national importance', he decreed that henceforth all excavations had to be done by Italian archaeologists. 'Petty persecutions' thundered Whitaker about his tormentor, professing himself 'disgusted' by the roadblocks put in his way. The rapport continued to disintegrate and by 1928, Gabrici's 'obstructionism' made earnest work on Motya impossible.

Sir Leonard Woolley, the British archaeologist, fared no better and aired his feud more publicly in two books, accusing Gabrici of 'rascality' over the export of antiquities in one and of uncredited plagiarizing of Woolley's field work on the Sabine settlement at Teano, between Rome and Naples, in another. Hardcastle, too, had his ups and downs with Gabrici. In a letter to Marconi after the conferral of the Crown of Italy honor, he confided that the Podestà of Girgenti 'was very kind to me, urging Rome to bestow an honour on me as early as 1925 (but Gabrici never thought to do so)'. And later, in July 1928, in another missive to Marconi, he confided that with regard to Arduino Colasanti becoming Superintendent of Antiquities in Rome 'having arrived at Girgenti in 1921, I immediately wished to excavate and to describe Akragas, but I lost all hope in 1924 as I told Colasanti in Rome [but] then this simpatico magician made...even Gabrici disappear and then suddenly you appeared and made things happen'.

# –13–

'GREEK RUINS AT GIRGENTI. RESTORATION OF HERAKLES TEMPLE', ran the headline of an illustrated report on April 21, 1924 in *The Times*. The article continued, 'The restoration of the Temple of Herakles has now been completed ... and the eight fluted columns make an imposing addition to the remarkable line of Doric temples on the seaward-facing wall of the famous Greek city of Akragas ... Hardcastle was warmly congratulated on his gift to Italy ... .' It was the third article to appear in the British press in just 24 months about this single restoration. Alexander was pleased and even more so about the task having now been finished. In the course of the work, fragments of an exquisite ceremonial vase decorated with pure gold had been unearthed and rushed off to the safety of the local museum.

But by then, Hardcastle already had other projects underway. There was so much more on his agenda! In fact, by March 1922, while awaiting the go-ahead to proceed on the Temple of Herakles, he had been granted approval by the Ministry in Rome to uncover and restore an ancient road paved in red and black bricks linking two plots of land, between the Grimaldi and Capraro farm properties, in the Valley.

His Italian by then was gradually improving. Although much of his correspondence was in English, he now felt confident enough to fire off some of his letters in Italian, untroubled by grammar and spelling. When messages were truly too complicated to render in that language, De Angelis stood by, styling himself as 'Hardcastle's secretary'.

The time had come, Alexander thought, to *also* come to grips with another ambitious project: the ancient perimeter wall that had encompassed the old city, running eight miles around Greek Akragas. Some of the stonework had simply crumbled with age. Some had been battered by the ripple effect of those earthquake tremors around the island, notably the ones of 1542, 1693 and 1908. Grazing goats had dislodged their share of masonry. More rocks had been pillaged by peasants to erect tool sheds and property boundaries. Whatever survived after such assaults was now smothered under a thick tangle of brush, weeds and indifference. It was high time for at least part of it to see the light of day.

When his overtures were seemingly put on the bottom of Palermo's in-tray, he turned to his local prefect, C. Reale: would *he* help force the pace a bit? The elaborate minuet resumed. Girgenti wrote to Palermo. Palermo wrote to Rome. And, at last, that sleeping giant, Rome, stirred. Hardcastle could now take off for a summer away from the blistering heat, reassured that matters were in place for a trouble-free launch in the autumn. He wanted to be on hand, in excitement, to watch the work. By November the last of the red tape was behind him. He had signed the requisite declaration vowing not to abscond with whatever antiquities came to light, and promising to cover the entire costs of the works and to take a back seat to glory. Officially, all clearance, excavation and restoration to the ancient walls of Akragas would appear carried out with funding by Rome. With that understood, Hardcastle reached for his chequebook: they would start on the eastern perimeter. The workforce was recruited, grateful for the employment and Alick wrote out the sum: 5000 Lire.

The authorities in Rome, Syracuse and Girgenti had good reason to begin feeling a bit uneasy. In Hardcastle's conversations and correspondence, a new word had started to creep in: 'our', as in '*our* excavations' and '*our* temples'. Was there a hidden agenda up his sleeve that had made him shift from '*your* excavations' and '*your* temples'? Agreeing to those rules helped clear the air. They put in black and white just what the terms were and Hardcastle obliged them with his signature. He was, after all, to confess to Paolo Orsi later on that, seized with excitement, he *had* undertaken 'small attempts at excavation' and that henceforth he 'would abstain'. It was a vow very challenging for him to stick to. With time, the Sicilian authorities *themselves* began to preface official correspondence of their own with the words 'Hardcastle's excavations'. Whatever way the nuances of language were to be read, one fact remained: Alexander now considered himself one of them. He stood apart, unique, from all the other foreign archaeologists who had come to the island from abroad. He was *not* there on a short-term whim. He was *not* there on a tightly-defined mission or project financed by either a university or a foreign government. Nor did he view his involvement as some sort of financial investment firmly anchored to later pay-back. He was there to stay. Permanently. And he was sharing the largesse from his own bank account with no strings attached, out of a love for classical history and the excitement of discovery. The dividends were purely intellectual and not monetary.

The momentum began to build towards the end of November 1923. In a letter to Ettore Gabrici in Palermo, Alexander came out into the open with a long-haboured dream:

> It is evident to me that Professor [Julius] Schübring was perfectly right when he wrote that Girgenti was, after Rome and Athens, 'the most important site of antiquity'. 'It would', he continued, 'be ... an honour ... to carry out larger excavations here. My general idea is to select a site as interesting and accessible as possible to the travellers of all nations who visit Girgenti, because if we can discover an important building such as the Greek theatre, there will be (I can assure you) no difficulty in collecting large sums for further researches from England and probably also from Americans who have just initiated extensive excavations at Carthage.[1] I therefore ... offer you ... a <u>preliminary</u> sum of fifty thousand lire to enable you ... to <u>search for</u> and then <u>excavate</u>

---

[1] Actually, he was referring to a Franco-American expedition to Tunisia directed by Byron Kuhn de Prorok to investigate the remains of buildings and artifacts showing evidence of the Carthaginians as practitioners of human sacrifice.

## Chapter 13

some important site such as the <u>theatre</u> or <u>agora</u>, both of which must have existed in Akragas … .

As New Year's Eve approached, Gabrici was able to report back that Rome would indeed accept the gracious offer of funding, to take explorations forward. Hardcastle, of course, already had a plan of attack clear in his head. We'll dig a 328-foot trench, to begin 'by the carob tree', he thought, and it will run down the slope.
Between resurrecting the eight columns of the Temple of Herakles, bringing to light a Greek road and embarking on a major clean-up of the ancient city walls, 1923 had been extremely busy. Further excavations brought the discovery of a Hellenistic or perhaps Archaic tempietto by the southeast corner of the Temple of Zeus, just west of the Herakles. The shovels had not remained stationary.

The wily farmers with modest land holdings in the Valley were rapidly developing inflationary responses to the munificent Englishman. When either Hardcastle or archaeologists visiting from Palermo cast their eyes for temporary expropriation over stony patches of Valley pastureland which might yield up promising discoveries, the savvy countrymen dug in to negotiate hard bargains. Suddenly the wisps of dried scrub on their land became costly forage for their goats and sheep. Their handful of almond and olive trees emerged as the source of untold wealth. Alick, irked and imperious, wrote Gabrici that one such person, a Mr Giuseppe Vella, had refused authorisation for them to excavate on one certain patch of the Vella property. Would Gabrici thus kindly attend to a temporary expropriation, overruling the intransigent farmer. Alexander would pay up for the brief loss of livelihood and for whatever damages to the land due to the dig. Without an exploratory excavation there, he stressed to Gabrici, a precise written plan of campaign could not be drawn up for submission to the Ministry in Rome for approval. It was an approval he hope would be forthcoming by the next autumn when the summer's heat had subsided. November of 1924, he thought, would be the optimum time for the archaeological hunt to begin in earnest. In point of fact, work began several months later.

In tandem with all the work in the Valley, the Villa Aurea over time was seeing a steady stream of visitors. Because it now belonged to an Englishman, his compatriots often felt an automatic claim on his time. Some people were welcome, others less so. Prince Umberto's courtesy call in September 1921 had been an honour. But a little over three and a half years later, early on the morning of May 9, 1924, a battleship eased into the Porto Empedocle harbour. On board was Benito Mussolini; it would be one of only two visits that he would ever pay to the island, stumping for support and trying to woo the stubborn bourgeoisie, so resistant to change, away from their sympathies for the mafia and into his camp. Garlands, banners, bunting and tooting horns all greeted the prime minister as he and his entourage made their way up from the port to Girgenti. For good measure, there was even an aerial and submarine escort! There were the official calls on the city fathers at the imposing town hall in Piazza Municipio, to renew hollow pledges to address the island's endemic problems of poverty and security. Then, in the afternoon, Mussolini was ushered off to see the sights, which concluded in the evening with a Pirandello comedy performed by actress Emma Grammatica's theatrical company. Grammatica was Italy's most celebrated actress following the recent death of Eleonora Duse. But before the performance, there was just time for a visit to the Valley of the Temples, escorted by Biagio Pace, the Sicilian-born archaeologist and art historian who was noted for his fascist sympathies. Accounts diverge on how it all went. The *Corriere della Sera* noted obsequiously that 'a most interesting visit to the temples of ancient Akragas took place'. Il Presidente took extreme interest in the very detailed tour, which lasted almost two hours. In a handed-down family account of the very same visit, however, Hardcastle wrote to his family in England that 'Mussolini came to see us'. His niece Felicité added that Alick reported having taken 'a dim view of him as he just walked round in silence with a rose in his mouth!' Hardcastle's private views pretty much tallied with those of the islanders. What had originally been envisaged as a two-week tour was pared down to five days. Nowhere on his itinerary did Mussolini experience the open-armed reception he hoped for.

The unvoiced chill was there, no question. Mussolini's mind at that moment was focussed elsewhere: plans shortly would be underway to dispatch an avowed enemy of the prime minister. On June 1, the socialist deputy Giacomo Matteotti stood up in the Chamber of Deputies in Rome and denounced Mussolini's fascists. He detailed the intimidations, the thuggery and the fraudulent methods used to achieve their majority vote and demanded that the election be voided. He ended darkly, saying 'and now get ready for my funeral'. Within ten days, the fascist hierarchy obliged and Matteotti was murdered, heralding the way for further political tension in the country. In Sicily, sulphur production that year continued to plummet, adding to local strife.

On a very personal level, Alexander had a setback of his own: he had, after three years' residence there, asked permission to extend the city water pipes down to the spigots of the Villa Aurea. His request was rebuffed. Not all, however, was looking arid. That talented young Veronese had arrived in Palermo and he was about to forge a memorable friendship with the Englishman. It was Pirro Marconi, of course.

# –14–

From the very outset, Pirro Marconi had his work cut out for himself. As assistant inspector of archaeological sites attached to the Archaeological Museum in Palermo in the early months of 1925, he was soon visiting the wealth of ancient Greek settlements throughout western Sicily. The job entailed ensuring that excavations and restorations were proceeding strictly according to instructions. It further meant assembling work teams, smoothing over whatever squabbles arose, making certain that temporary land expropriation documents were in order before digging on private property,[1] overseeing the cataloguing of discovered relics, writing up the findings for publication, reporting back to Paolo Orsi in Syracuse.

If Marconi arrived in Sicily with a hint of youthful brashness – he was still in his twenties – and began questioning the methods of his elders, that soon toned down and gave way to diplomatic finesse. Busy years lay ahead and there was no point in getting off to a prickly start. Humouring the headstrong Hardcastle, too, required the conciliatory approach.

Alexander was unshakeably convinced that a theatre, as an integral part of a rich Greek town, *had* to be there, somewhere, ripe and waiting for discovery. Akragas was no exception. It existed and it *had* to be found. On late afternoon strolls, paying visits to his Sicilian friends, Hardcastle would tap his metal-tipped alpenstock on their doors to announce his presence. The opening gambit was always the same: '*Il teatro! Dove sarà il teatro?*'[2]

Marconi, by now at Girgenti regularly, could do nothing more than sigh heavily. Leash had to be given to the Valley's greatest benefactor. Later, he could get back to his own agenda. Writing to Orsi, Marconi reported that 'results from the principal excavations are still going slowly and aren't very heartening;[3] they are deep and shovelling [out the dirt] is arduous … . I've hired six lads to carry the rubble off to an inconspicuous site away from the trenches. I think sadly how much could be accomplished by this team elsewhere … but Captain Hardcastle is all for the theatre, so the bulk of the work must remain on that. But I hope that in another week or two we'll have our answers and if the results are as I pessimistically fear they'll be, namely "no", then we can focus on other

---

[1] Authorisation was frequently achieved with a straggly 'X' from the illiterate.
[2] Trans: The theatre! Where do you suppose the theatre is?
[3] Hardcastle himself had chosen the site of the excavation, immediately to the north of the old San Nicola monastery. There was momentary excitement when workers struck some circular walls. They were determined to be part of an ancient aqueduct, however.

matters.' Marconi would later remember it as 'this useless hunt'. He went on to say to Orsi that 'Nonetheless, a lot of material has been collected. Today on site, including myself, there is the enormous sum of 50 workers.[4] I think all of Girgenti dreams of living on Hardcastle's 50,000 Lire. I've found it necessary to take this matter in hand , otherwise Hardcastle's secretary will send me one hundred more! I will no longer, for any reason, accept workers who think they have "pull". In fact ... I intend to start weeding out the excess. The situation here in Girgenti is rather tricky and I don't want, under any circumstance, to bow to the *sistemi meridionali*, whereby a job is considered theirs because of a favour owed or a personal recommendation.'

For Marconi, this was all sort of a baptism by fire and his patience was sorely tried with Hardcastle, on the one hand, pushing for the impossible and the local labourers, on the other, scurrying around him like voracious picnic ants, eager for the crumbs of work. He did not lose his composure. Meanwhile, Alick had turned his energies to yet more frustrating challenges.

Around that time, Luigi Pirandello was Girgenti's most celebrated son. After studies in Palermo and Bonn, he decamped to the literary life of Rome and embarked on his own prolific writing career. Newspaper and magazine articles, novels, essays, poetry, short stories and plays all flowed fast from his pen. And although most of his professional life was spent in the capital, Pirandello's ties with Girgenti, remained strong and particularly with his birthplace, in the *contrada* called 'Caos' on the edge of town. When he could not visit, friends kept him abreast of news from home. Inevitably, that included the doings of the curious Englishman in their midst.

Many travellers to Sicily were captivated by the omnipresent spectacle of goats. They were *everywhere*. One English visitor gushed that 'these animals with their satyr-like countenances and musky odour ... seem to fit in with the landscape. The goats of Girgenti are a race apart, larger, silkier than those of other places, with broad, twisted horns and aristocratic airs. They bend their comely heads to crop the flowery grass among the temples.' But, alas, not only the grass. Therein lay the problem as Hardcastle saw it.

He winced at the picturesque postcards with the artfully posed creatures, invariably in the foreground. He cringed when, in real life, these dubious desecrators reared up onto their hind limbs against a temple pillar or wall, the better to tease weeds growing out of the crevices, pulling out mortar as they munched. For Hardcastle it was open war. He arranged for wire fencing to be run up around the more fragile ruins, he pleaded with the *contadini* to steer their flocks elsewhere and he paid for thickets of bushes and trees to be planted. Partly to enhance the beauty of the place, but also to provide the goats with less threatening forage. The Girgentini were somewhere between confused and bemused: did **all** foreigners get so upset by mere goats? And surely, as master milk-makers, weren't the goats far more important than some pile of old rocks?

---

[4] Built into the expenditures was an average of 210 Lire per month for drinking water for each of the crew.

## Chapter 14

When the gossip about Hardcastle's pitched battles reached Pirandello's ears, it was to be instant and rich fodder for his pen and ripe for a short story, *'Il Capretto Nero'*. [5] Pirandello's novella is the tale of Mr Charles Trockley, a long-time English resident of Girgenti. He is a precise fellow with firm convictions (he doesn't like goats). Like Hardcastle, Trockley enjoys his evening strolls among the temples. Also like Hardcastle, his compatriots come calling. It falls to Trockley, in fact, to accompany one such young visitor, Miss Ethel Holloway, around the Greek ruins. Mademoiselle, however, is immediately distracted by an enchanting little black kid prancing about. She orders its capture, buys it and instructs that it be held for her until her return to England when she can send for it. No prizes for guessing who Pirandello designates as the goat's interim caretaker. Although the playwright dressed up the Englishman as a British vice consul, everyone in Girgenti knew exactly who Trockley *really* was. The gentle spoof gave the locals a harmless laugh. Alexander's reaction was not recorded.

What was not a chapter of fiction in the spring of 1925 was that Hardcastle was indeed expecting an important lady visitor from England and her even more important husband. By then Alexander had had to digest the goat problem as a fact of life; his hunt for the theatre had quietly been shelved; other excavations had resumed.

Back in England, meanwhile, King George V caught a cold returning from the theatre in London one damp and bitter night in February 1925. Long years as a smoker had already taken a toll on his lungs. His cold quickly escalated into influenza, then turned into bronchitis. The king took to bed, hoping it would all pass speedily. The illness seesawed for awhile; when his condition finally stabilized sufficiently, the bevy of court doctors urged convalescence on a Mediterranean cruise aboard the royal yacht. Reluctantly the King bowed to orders; it was the first time in fifteen years that he would absent himself from home to take a foreign holiday. Arrangements were meticulously drawn up and the royal train with eleven cars bore him southwards to Genoa on the Riviera. Hardcastle was duly informed that the King would be calling shortly and that he, Hardcastle, would be doing the honours there in the Valley. With Queen Mary at his side, George V boarded the HMY **Victoria and Albert III,** late the afternoon of March 20. Built in 1899, the vessel was the largest and most magnificent royal yacht in Europe, destined to serve three monarchs. Given the mild weather, the party called in at several Italian ports, reaching their final destination of Palermo towards the middle of April. When the grandees of Palermo had all entertained the monarchs, the plan was to lift anchor for Porto Empedocle the night of April 13. No one had reckoned, however, on a possible change in the weather. The storm clouds gathered, pouring down buckets. It was no time to risk the king's health once again and so he and Queen Mary stayed put in the Sicilian capital. A photograph in the royal archives at Windsor show the two attending a hastily convened luncheon party at the palace of the Gangi princes in Palermo on April

---

[5] Trans: 'The Black Kid'. Between 1922-1937, in addition to all his other works, Pirandello produced 15 volumes of short stories under the regular title of 'Novelle Per Un' Anno'. 'Il Capretto Nero' appeared in the second volume, published in 1925.

14. The Queen as ever wore a tailored three-quarter length linen suit for the occasion. Alexander and the crestfallen city fathers made do in Girgenti that day with the next best thing: a small party from the royal entourage that had been dispatched southwards to soothe bruised feelings over the sudden change of plans. Among them was Lord Dawson of Penn, the King's attending physician throughout the trip. It fell to Alexander to escort the group through the Greek temples and point out ongoing excavations in which he was heavily involved. Later, afternoon tea was served to the Englishmen out on the Villa Aurea terrace with luscious little cakes brought down the hill from Girgenti's poshest pasticceria, Zarcone. Hardcastle gently suggested to Dawson that the King should come to winter among the ruins where the weather was *normally* magnificent.

One blueblood who *did* make it that same month on a more clement day of sunlight was Lord Howard who moored his yacht at Porto Empedocle and made his way up the Valley to pay a call, on an unspoken mission. Harry had an inkling of what was going on and gave an amusing account of the day at the Villa Aurea:

> … about Geoffrey Howard. He came to Villa Aurea in April 1925 and as I tell … the story … you ought to guess gradually … why he came. A Howard takes over all those posts and those duties which have to do with peerage, primogeniture, precedence, privilege, etc. So much for G. Howard. Now for Alick. They approached one another like two engineers tunnelling from opposite sides of a mountain. In April 1925 Alick had a card and a letter from the Hotel des Temples from one Geoffrey Howard … and about now I began to scent something in the wind. Alick had been corresponding with the Home Secretary and told me he was the minister who allowed English subjects to accept foreign orders. So by the time the Howards arrived I saw what was going on. I knew. Alick did not know anything. Howard did not know that I knew. It being a delicate matter I said nothing, then or later. And Alick never knew then or later why Howard called.
>
> However call he did and brought Mrs [sic] Howard and Mr Leif Jones. We gave them English tea. Mr Leif Jones played a quiet part quietly, and no doubt while we were talking his eye was running over the furniture and pricing it! After tea Alick led them into the garden … .

About a month later permission came to Alick from the Home Office to wear the insignia of a Commendatore of the Corona d'Italia. Mr Howard and party had come all across the island on duty and reported favourably of Alick's house and grounds and deportment and company and general fitness to sustain the honour of England.

# −15−

As the mid-1920s approached, Hardcastle moved further afield. It had not taken him long to note that Sicilian summers bordered on the unbearable. Temperatures hovered well over a stifling 95°F for weeks, if not months, on end. If he and his brother were to have any respite at all, he'd have to find it further north. Better yet if there were a project to accompany the summer migration, something to keep him intellectually engaged.

Alexander had long admired his countryman, George Dennis and shared many of his enthusiasms. The two were similarly drawn to Sicily. But Hardcastle was <u>now</u> about to be swayed by Dennis's other earlier passion: the Etruscan countryside surrounding Viterbo, to the northwest of Rome. 'I owe all my interest [in the place] to my compatriot George Dennis', he admitted. Dennis had first come to that area, known as Etruria, in June-July of 1842, in his late 20s, well before Hardcastle was even born. By the next summer, Dennis had already visited Etruria three times. Travelling back and forth between home in England and these parts, he continued his fact-finding missions, taking meticulous notes, which, in 1848, culminated in a book, 'The Cities and Cemeteries of Etruria'. It described in detail the early Etruscan settlements of central Italy and was reckoned to be the definitive work on the subject in those years. But by then, Dennis was restlessly on the move, exploring other Italian interests.

He made a first trip to Sicily in late 1847 and travelled there again in 1852 and 1857. He began amassing new material for a further book, 'A Handbook For Travellers in Sicily'. Research and publication was severely slowed down, though, because of his diplomatic duties, which kept him in British Guyana. Visits to the island could only be scheduled during breaks in Europe. Sicily was clearly to his liking. In those days, it was an important place for the English: the trickle of visitors there was steady. Business ties were solid. Representing these interests were eleven British vice-consulates dotted around Sicily. A consular post was *just* the sort of plum that would suit Dennis nicely, allowing him to pursue his passion for classical digs. Alas, that plum did not materialise immediately. After the false hope of a posting to Syracuse, he was at last allowed to leave his pestilential outpost in South America in 1864 only to be sent to Benghazi, a 'dreary dreary moorland!', a 'barren barren shore!' In a mournful letter to his publisher in London, he added: 'I hope I am not doomed to a long exile in this Ulubrae'. After four years in north Africa, the Dennises moved on to Smyrna. Finally, he was rewarded with Palermo in the late spring of 1870 and happily packed his bags to move on from the eastern Mediterranean to his congenial new setting. He and his wife Nora would make the grand diplomatic residence in Palermo their home for the next nine years. If Dennis could divide his affection evenly between two distinct eras, the Greeks and the Etruscans, so too could Hardcastle! His sights fixed on Viterbo.

Presumably, by the summer of 1924, Alexander and 'HRH', as he often called Harry, began their first trek north out of Girgenti. Parsimoniously, he took along his Villa Aurea printed stationery from Sicily, crossing out the southern address and penning in his new summer headquarters, The Grand Hotel, Viterbo. The first foray was clearly a reconnaissance mission and the Englishman liked what he saw. He was relieved that the barometer assured more tolerable temperatures. But if the Viterbo countryside were to become his warm-weather command post, he'd have to find more suitable living arrangements than a hotel suite. As in Girgenti, Hardcastle preferred peace, quiet and privacy, removed from the prying curiosity of the town folk.

The many-branched Balestra family was a notable name around Viterbo. In 1902, one of them, Mario Balestra, had teamed up with another local man, Luigi Rossi Danielli, to explore an intriguing theatre at Ferento, five and a half miles north of Viterbo, just off the Via Teverina. The wellborn Rossi Danielli had financed out of his own pocket some of the early excavations there, clearing around the orchestra, the pit and the scaena, bringing to light some magnificent marble sculptures. It would then be another Balestra, a cousin of Mario's named Filippo, to show sympathy for the archaeological interests of these newly-arrived foreigners. Filippo Balestra owned a sprawling property in the foothills of the Cimino Mountain range, just to the east of Viterbo. On it was his own patrician Villa Palanzana. But there was abundant acreage left over on which to build another villa assuring privacy to both. With that in mind, on July 19, 1925, Filippo Balestra sat down in the office of Anselmo Anselmi, a famed local notary and bibliophile, side by side with the Hardcastle brothers to draw up a curious contract. 'Desirous to possess a quiet and isolated spot on which to build a little house and pass idle hours amidst the greenery of trees and the silence of the countryside', it began poetically, Balestra's contract expressed his willingness to give over, outright, a ten-acre parcel of land to the east of town in the *contrada* known as Palanzana. It lay at the foot of a handsome hill and had rolling pasture land and some woods. It was not a proper sale, for Balestra could not bear to part from any of his lands. No money would be exchanged for the land itself, and the Hardcastles were free to build a villa at their own expense. At the end of their natural lives, however, the property, including the house, would revert wholly to the Balestra family. For his part, Balestra undertook to allow cows – but no goats! – grazing rights to the land only when the Hardcastles were <u>not</u> in residence. He further promised that when the brothers planted their gardens at Palanzana (Alexander was nurturing a growing interest in flowers and bushes, by this time) they would remain untrampled by animals. The contract revealed one further interesting fact: the two brothers had cut their sister, Mira Francisca, into the partnership. Her name appears even though she was not present at the signing formalities in Anselmi's office. Thus not all the bridges were burned with family. The reversion clause did not trouble the three Hardcastles, for none had married and there were no offspring to provide for.

*Chapter 15*

*Entrance to Hardcastle's Villa Palanzana, with his coat of arms over the doorway. (Photo: the author)*

With the formalities now behind him, Alexander was now free to begin building his first and very own house, entirely from scratch. He would call his three-story home alternatively the Villa or Villino Palanzana. To the viterbesi, though, it was simply 'la casa degli inglesi'.[1] It was constructed in blocks of *piperino,* the mottled grey stone native to Viterbo. Inside as well as out, the structure could only be described as Victorian Gothic. As an architectural style, it did have its fans in Italy and so was not entirely out of place. The stone-framed windows tapered into points, an ornately-chiselled staircase led upstairs and stencilled embellishments ran the length of the upper part of the indoor walls. On the ground floor, several spacious and high-ceilinged reception rooms and studies led one into another, all well-ventilated for the hot months and kept cool by the tiled flooring. Upstairs were the sleeping quarters and bathrooms. Between July when the

---

[1] Trans: House of the Englishmen.

document was signed and December, work evidently proceeded at record pace. Stone quarries lay very near by and probably Balestra was able to quickly steer a full work team to the site from a construction job he had just completed elsewhere in town. In all, the house had 12 spacious rooms. By the end of 1925, Alexander was proudly able to affix a chiselled stone lintel above the front entranceway which read: 'DOM HARDCASTLE MCMXXV' and just beneath it, an adaptation of his father's coat of arms. His father's shield featured three castle towers and three leopard heads on a chevron. Underneath were the words DEUS MIHI MUNIMEN, God is my fortress. Alexander's, instead, bore a single tower and nothing else. Before long, neighbours were turning up in their carriages to inspect the newcomers and take afternoon tea under the oak grove not far from the new house.

*Interior view, today, of the stone staircase at the Villa Palazana, outside Viterbo.*
*(Photo: the author)*

*Chapter 15*

All in all, it was an exceedingly busy year. Ongoing excavations in his beloved Valley of the Temples were in high gear. He had single-handedly overseen the building at breakneck speed of his new home in the north. And now he was beginning to be captured by something entirely new: Ferento. The theatre which eluded him so frustratingly back in Girgenti would now rise from the rubble in the north, just outside Viterbo.

*View of the theatre at Ferento.*

## −16−

'Civitas splendidissima Ferentiensium' was the phrase of one anonymous second-century AD writer describing Ferento. Conquered by the Romans in 310 BC, it had been the site of an early Etruscan settlement. Thanks to the rich agricultural land and to its strategic position near the Tiber River, the city flourished and grew, sprawling seventy-five acres out to the edge of a plateau north of Viterbo. Massive walls rose up around the city, protecting its inhabitants from marauders. Emperor Vespasian's modest-born wife, Flavia Domitilla, came from here, as did the short-reigning Emperor Otho.

Its natural resources soon brought many of the trappings of affluence: temples dedicated to Fortuna and Salus, goddesses respectively of fate and of health and prosperity, as well as a forum decorated with 'colossal figures', as Vitruvius recalled. Stone bas-reliefs adorned further buildings, while thermal spas were brightened with coloured paving. But the jewel in the crown lay elsewhere, built during the Augustan era, between the 1$^{st}$ century BC and 1$^{st}$ century AD. 'The grand monument at Ferento is the theatre', wrote George Dennis. 'In its perfect state it must have been a truly imposing edifice; even now, though all the winds of heaven play through its open arches, it is a most majestic ruin with every advantage of situation to increase its effect on the senses. For it stands on the brink of a precipice, overhanging a wooded and picturesque ravine, amid solitude, ruin and desolation, where for centuries man has left his dwelling to the falcon, the owl, the bat, the viper, and the lizard, and where his foot or voice now rarely calls forth echoes.'

Resplendent in his white linen jacket and with a wide-brimmed panama to shield him from the sun, Alexander travelled out from the Grand Hotel and was at once dazzled and dismayed by what he saw: just enough of its handsome arches, its 131-foot long scena (stage) and semi-circular cavea, or seating area, survived to envisage what it all would look like if restored. Overall, though, he saw sad neglect. Vague forms sheathed in a tangled mess of vegetation. A hinted-at history of plunder. Just like Girgenti.

In writing his book on Etruria, Dennis had ardently hoped to draw ever more compatriots to see the Etruscan wonders. It tallied perfectly with Hardcastle's aspirations for Girgenti. Alick now felt that by restoring the theatre, he, too, might excite the attention of the English.

A site of interest ever since Renaissance times, Ferento had offered rich pickings over the decades for antiquity thieves. Relics had evaporated in the direction of the United States. Restoration work was perennially at the mercy of available money - state or private. Surveillance was virtually non-existent. When funds were available, work limped

## Chapter 16

forward, one patch at a time. When allotted money was used up, work stopped. And then, the Roman remains would sink back into oblivion awaiting a new financial kiss of life. The old story.

Beginning in 1901, *Viterbesi* Luigi Rossi Danielli and Mario Balestra had privately undertaken explorations of the theatre to determine how much was intact. They uncovered about half of the lower part of the scena and had identified medieval-era additions to the complex, including the remains of a tower. Shortly afterwards, in 1909 it fell to Edoardo Galli of the Florence Superintendency to carry the baton.[1] Florence used its own injection of official funds to study the layout of Ferento in detail and where the theatre stood in relation to the thermal baths and the decumanus and other salient points of the city. They had uncovered a large part of the cavea, as well as the remains of a church built there at a later stage in history. Then its funds, too, were exhausted.

As Hardcastle stood before the ruins in 1925, on that very first visit, he took off his metal-rimmed glasses and rubbed his eyes. He saw how things *might* be. How 'his' theatre *could* once more be. Pietro Romanelli would soon be earmarked to directly conduct the Ferento excavations, with Costantino Zei, the local honorary inspector, as his on-the-spot, right-hand man. The Rome-born Romanelli was 36 at the time and an experienced archaeologist. He had taken his degree from Rome University in 1911, then promptly enrolled in the Italian School of Archaeology. He was 23 years old when Paribeni invited him along on a mission to southern Anatolia, in Turkey. In 1919, Romanelli went to Libya where for four years, he oversaw the excavations at Leptis Magna. His book on the magnificent Roman remains there came out twenty-four months after his return to Italy in 1923. On repatriation, he was named Superintendent of Antiquities for Rome, which in point of fact, also meant Etruria. Scholarly, religious and slightly owlish in his thick-rimmed eyeglasses, Romanelli's interests in such things as ancient building ornamentation did not always coincide with Hardcastle's leanings. What was more, he was older than Marconi in Sicily. There would be none of the paternal feelings here that Alexander possibly felt towards Marconi. Romanelli would make his name in the coming years with excavations at Tarquinia, Ostia and Rome's Palatine Hill, among other places. Right now, though, the spotlight was on Ferento.

Nonetheless, it was to Roberto Paribeni, once again, that Alexander instinctively addressed his immediate thoughts. 'Being now a resident every summer at Viterbo',[2] he wrote on July 5th 1925, 'I am anxious to restore this splendid and unique theatre for the benefit of visitors of all nations … For this purpose I have the pleasure of offering to the

---

[1] Viterbo, to its regret, in those years fell under the administrative aegis of the Florence superintendency. Indeed, Florence removed eight marble sculptures of the muses inspired by Greek works of the 4th century, including Erato, Calliope, Euterpe, Melpomene, Thalia, Cleo, Tersicore and Urania from Ferento. A long feud ensued between Viterbo and Florence. Lopsided swaps were suggested. Payments were proposed. It was only in the mid-1980s after 82 years that cooler heads prevailed and the eight sculptures quietly returned to Viterbo. They are now housed in the Rocca d'Albornoz National Archaeological Museum.

[2] This letter, in point of fact, was written two weeks *before* he and his brother had signed the land contract with Filippo Balestra.

Government a first instalment of twenty-five thousand lire (£25,000) without any conditions of any kind.' Clearly, Paribeni replied immediately, for Hardcastle wrote him again ten days later, on July 15$^{th}$: 'Thank-you for your letter of July 11$^{th}$ – I hope you will be able to begin the excavation of the theatre of Ferento, <u>without waiting to decide</u> the questions of the removal of the medieval tower + the restitution of objects from Florence – there will be plenty of time to decide, while we are excavating the remainder (about one half) of the cavea and scena, still covered with <u>earth + vegetation</u> – which I should like to begin removing as soon as possible, please.' Alick's long military training was not easily erased: one was to get on with the job quickly. No procrastination. Paribeni took the train north to confer directly with the restless Englishman, then returned to report directly to his superiors in Rome. 'Notwithstanding my considerable reservations about seeing the place used for performances … . I believe that his offer is acceptable and that excavations could begin forthwith. 25,000 Lire will perhaps not suffice to complete [the work] but I am confident that obtaining further help will not be impossible.' By now, the Hardcastle name was familiar around the Ministry of Education and his record in Sicily proven. A reply came back quickly to Paribeni: 'Agreed. Draft a *good* press release for the newspapers … [remembering, too] all of the Captain's other praiseworthy deeds.' Jumping the gun, the ex-Royal Engineer had, by August 5$^{th}$, *already* dispatched a squad of labourers to cut a proper access road through from the Via Teverina into the archaeological site! Now that the approach was assured, work could begin.

## −17−

If Alexander seemed itchy, it was with good reason. His dreams of uncovering a theatre at Girgenti earlier that year had been bruisingly dashed. (In a letter to Marconi years later, he admitted the venture had been an 'obsessione infantile' [sic].)[1] Now, Ferento offered far better prospects: a theatre was there already, albeit in ruins, plain for all to see.

In the world of Italian archaeology, Hardcastle was now increasingly a familiar name. He was proving a valuable asset not to be sidelined. What was more, he had earned a bit of celebrity a few months before, attracting members of the British royal entourage to his 'back yard' on the island. The Valley was further enhanced: Girgenti now counted six hotels. The latest, which opened in 1926, was the Grand Hotel et Agrigentum, built along the Viale della Vittoria on property owned by Ignazio Altieri's family. Boasting all the latest conveniences, it was a welcome new venue for visitors. By the end of 1925, thanks in good measure to Hardcastle, 2030 visitors had flocked in to see the eight uprighted columns of Herakles. Maybe he could turn up the wattage at Ferento as well.

Right off, road-making into the site struck it lucky: four Roman tombs were found just by the embankment. It was a promising start. By October, as Alexander saw his new home rise from the building site at Palanzana, so too did he see the tangle at Ferento disappear. That month, Paribeni recorded notable progress: 'all is proceeding well and with good results and [we are] spreading out at the express wish of [Hardcastle] who seemingly appears willing to offer more money [to the project].'

It was high time, thought Paribeni, to put Hardcastle up for an official decoration in gratitude for his generosity to Italian archaeology. Maybe the Cross of the Order of Saints Maurice and Lazarus, he mused. This was normally the honour earmarked for foreign subjects. Perhaps unknown to Paribeni, movement was already afoot towards decorating Alexander. An even more prestigious medal was contemplated. It would be another twenty-seven months, however, before the royal decree was made public and a further few months before Hardcastle actually received the decoration in Girgenti, entitling him to call himself Commendatore.

Before long, Alexander was talking about a further refuelling of 25,000 Lire for Ferento. Winter was approaching though, and Girgenti beckoned. The records do not say when exactly he left Viterbo, to return south. But as a rule, he did not like work that he was financing to proceed in his absence. He liked the *frisson* of the dig and he liked to keep a watchful eye on the expenditure of his own money. In all likelihood, Ferento was put on hold during the winter period of 1925-1926.

---

[1] Trans: childish obsession

Even if there was a halt to excavations, that did not mean that Costantino Zei, too, was put on hold. As the undergrowth was wrested free, Zei was able to study the surviving structures more attentively. In a long-winded letter penned to Paribeni, Zei made his recommendations. Support walls either needed to be rebuilt or otherwise shored up. If they weren't, other areas of the theatre would simply collapse. The law of good luck could not be relied on indefinitely. Just as worrying were the seismic tremors that periodically struck central Italy and that had affected Ferento in the past. Who could predict when the next quake would occur? By the summer of 1926, Zei pleaded for the western wall flanking the scena to be next on the list: 'Hardcastle is ever willing to carry out at his expense these important and costly works', he reported to Rome. If all the walls were repaired and the niches of the eight muses made sound once more, the local inspector fantasized the return of the sculptures to their original site. Long discussions then ensued about the brickwork. In reconstructing, would it be better to faithfully replicate what had vanished with the ravages of time? That is, to have a perfect match of old and new, a seamless blend. Or was it instead desirable to deliberately show the contrast between yesterday and today, using new building blocks that were patently different? Zei's vote was for contrast: '[the brick] shapes, sizes and nature all faithfully carried out, letting [the viewer] clearly see [what is] new... .' He made this known to both Paribeni <u>and</u> Hardcastle.

The latter did not take it lying down and promptly fired *his* views off to Rome: 'Today I received a letter from Professor Zei to say it is necessary to execute the restoration at Ferento 'unicamente a mattoni', but I think there are two schools of thought, and two different ideas about restoration. The <u>German</u> archaeologists say that new modern pieces must be <u>clearly distinguished</u> from the old (original) pieces; but at Oxford University I was told that this is <u>not</u> necessary, because the new pieces can be stamped marked with the year (1926) in order to distinguish them from the old pieces and it is better for <u>artistic</u> reasons to make the new work <u>resemble</u> the old, as much as <u>possible</u>. Naturally I leave the question to you; but I hope you will try to restore the theatre at Ferento to its <u>original appearance</u> as far as possible ...' In citing Oxford, perhaps Alick was thinking specifically about Sir Arthur John Evans and the palace of Knossos where skillful and imaginative restoration and not mere conservation was adopted for collapsed walls, staircases and paving.

Interestingly, the issue had not arisen noticeably at Girgenti when the eight columns of Herakles went back up. Admittedly, the original 'ingredients' were all to hand and there had been no need for modern infill. Ironically, one of the rare voices raised in dissent over Herakles came from one of Alexander's very own countrymen, Edward Hutton, who sniffed: 'I could have wished them undisturbed.'

By the end of July 1926, the matter at Ferento had not been resolved entirely amicably. Alick again picked up his pen to Paribeni in Rome 'I have visited Ferento ... and ... hope you will be able to reconstruct the arches ... using the very numerous pieces of "peperino" lying on the site, ready "patinate e cifrate". A small piece has been already restored "a mattoni", but it does not harmonize well with the peperino and we fear that if many and larger pieces a mattoni are inserted, the noble appearance of the arches will become ridiculous.'

Impatiently the letter went on, pushing for progress elsewhere: fortifying the façade wall, which threatened to topple outwards with the winter weather. Erecting a small home for the on-premise custodian, to be built over a place to display the growing number of relics emerging from the earth. When he discovered the site foreman off on an unannounced holiday, Alexander railed at that, too. He questioned price estimates at every turn, even challenging the cost of barbed wire fencing. Nothing slipped his attention. But happily for him, the authorities finally bent when it came to bricks versus stone. By mid-September, he noted to Rome that 'the restoration is progressing well. One new arch has been completed with blocks of peperino and looks very dignified.' He instructed that a notice board at the junction of the Via Teverina should be made in iron, not wood, for greater durability, adding that 'You will agree that it is always advisable to awaken public interest in such glorious ruins of the past'.

It was just as well that the Hardcastles were not in Girgenti the summer of 1926. That August, 27 months after Mussolini's first lightening trip south, Augusto Turati was dispatched to Sicily: much had been promised in the way of betterments to the islanders, but very little actually delivered. Now Turati, who earlier that year had risen to secretary general of the fascist party, taking over from Roberto Farinacci, came on another empty-handed mission to the sceptical Sicilians: he was there on the Duce's behalf to muster support from the reluctant locals. He would pledge Rome's support on one of the main festering grievances important to the locals: the dismantling of the large estates for redistribution to the needy. Turati wielded a symbolic shovel for the press and the cameras. It fooled no one and did little to shake the islanders out of their *siciliatude*.

From the furrows of the hinterland, Turati proceeded on to Girgenti where a requisite visit to the Temples was on his itinerary. The two English brothers, of course, were far from the scene, busied in the north with Ferento.

The secretary general's trip did not win over the Sicilians any more than Mussolini's visit had two years earlier. But stealthily, the mood was changing. Swollen national pride was leaving its imprint on *some* Girgentini. The local bully boys, the *squadristi*, were flexing their muscles more and more, feeling much legitimised by the secretary general's visit.

Administering castor oil, a favourite punishment for fascism's enemies, forced down the throats of perceived adversaries as a matter of course; oaths of loyalty to the Duce had to be sworn publicly before all performances at the Regina Margherita theatre could begin; parades and the shouting of slogans were regular events; youngsters were herded out to perform callisthenics in the piazza; all anti-government literature was suppressed; uniformed sympathizers swaggered up and down the Via Atenea, chests swollen, jaws protruding in close approximation of their balding leader in Rome. Most tellingly, a one-way ticket to *confine* –internment – awaited those who broadcast political objections slightly too loudly.

From time to time, they had their comeuppance and their boorish behaviour was met head on. They didn't always take it lightly. At one ball in the Circolo Empedocle, a fascist notable's bid for a dance with a young lady was cold-shouldered by the signorina. Her *carnet de bal* was taken up, she explained stiffly, 'by the *marchese*'. To which the fascist replied crudely, likening the marquis to venereal disease. A far cry from the well-mannered dance-floor patter in Lampedusa's 'The Leopard', where such vulgarities would never have been uttered. Hardcastle would be confronted with the subtle new shadings of change upon his return in the late autumn.

# −18−

By late autumn, Alick and Harry were back in Sicily. Nearly five years had gone by since their arrival and Alexander was increasingly certain of one thing: when the time came, Girgenti was where he wanted to end his days and to be buried. The Bonamorone Cemetery on the extreme northeastern side of town had opened in 1922. It was so new that not many of the plots had yet been spoken for. Hardcastle could choose his gravesite where he wanted, a gift of the city. True to form, he opted for the remotest spot possible. Just like the sitings of the Villas Aurea and Palanzana! In death, as in life, he would enjoy privacy and apartness. But he chose a far corner on the eastern side of the cemetery for a further reason. Just beyond the high cemetery walls, on the slopes below, stood the temple to the Greek goddess Demeter, deity of earthly plenty, as well as another ancient rock sanctuary devoted to her worship.

As one of the early excavations that he financed, Demeter had had him in her grip almost from the start. She embodied the bounty of the soil and its fertility. In mythology, she was the sister of Zeus, by whom she had Persephone. But when this daughter was abducted by Hades, lord of the underworld, Demeter despaired as she hunted high and low for her missing child. Zeus then commanded the release of Persephone by Hades. Thereafter, with Persephone at her side, Demeter caused the earth to flourish once more, throughout the summer months. And it was in honour of this chthonic deity, of the soil, that ancient Akragas built a sizeable temple in c. 470 BC on the eastern slope of the valley, beneath the Bonamorone Cemetery.

It counted two round sacrificial altars on the northern flank of the temple, the larger of which measured 9.8 feet in diameter. Alick's excavations there yielded a rich haul of votive lamps and handsome lion-headed spouts that had once adorned the gutter of the temple. With time and probable pillaging, the temple eroded and the medieval Norman Church of San Biagio went up on the site, incorporating some of the surviving rubble of the temple into its structure. San Biagio literally rested on the ancient grate-like stone foundations of the temple. As with most other sites, earth and vegetation took over, erasing all vestiges and all memory of the Demeter origins.

Hardcastle's push to clear the undergrowth suddenly put it back on the map and enabled the archaeologists to study the remains more closely. But what captured him perhaps most – remember, he was a military engineer by training – was the *approach* to Demeter's temple and the earlier sanctuary, set cave-like into the nearby hillside. Deep chariot ruts gouged the stone road -- very clear evidence of the much vehicular to-ing and fro-ing up this rugged artery to propitiate the goddess. He studied the ancient track marks and punctiliously measured them. With almost childish glee, he later would catch Marconi out. Like his grandfather decades earlier, who spent a great deal of his time in Girgenti measuring the girths of Greek columns, Alick was a stickler about inches and centimetres: the correct breadth 'between chariot wheels was 1.436 metres (4 feet 7 inches) and *not* 1.37', (4 feet 5 inches) as Marconi reported. With good humour, Marconi graciously conceded his mistake in print and thanked his benefactor. Alexander made a further discovery about the chariot tracks. They were a standard width and that width *also* corresponded in modern day closely to the gauge of railroad cars. He was very proud of that 'discovery' and never failed to tell friends about it.[1]

All these fond associations with the Demeter digs, then, made it almost imperative that Hardcastle take a few extra steps over his burial place. He had a stone mason at Bonamorone knock out a small rectangular window in the cemetery wall near where his head would later lie, as if to assure himself a view for eternity. And there were other details as well. There would be no monstrous sculptured marble monuments, so dear to the tastes of bereaving Italians, to paperweight his grave. No lachrymose angels, no garlanded crucifixes. No ornate prose would clutter up his afterlife. Just a plain slab of stone with his name and dates.[2] Two cypress trees would stand sentry nearby, as well as a magnolia and a little patch of grass that would remind visitors of this man's greened birthplace. The little window would tell the world, without words, that Alexander Hardcastle lay – vigilantly- over his adored Valley of the Temples.

As the 1925 'campaign' drew to a close, Alick turned to a local quarryman to produce a small marble tablet to affix to the base of the Demeter site. It read:

**1925 Excavations carried out by Captain Alex.r Hardcastle
with the express approval of Baron G. Celauro**

It was not stirred by vanity so much as an example-setting appeal to all landowners in the Valley, such as the Baron Giovanni Celauro di Sant'Alberta, to cooperate with all future excavations. Seeing their names immortalized in marble, it was hoped, would inspire others to speed up the temporary expropriations of their land in the cause of archaeology. Or, as Alexander himself put it, 'The purpose [of the tablet] is to please the proprietors of Girgenti who, in the past, have opposed all excavations. Now they are becoming more amicable.' It was something he had done before at the sites of other projects with the

---

[1] As late as 1929, Alick was writing to Antiquity: 'There were recently many letters in The Times about the origin of our strange railway gauge of 4 feet 8 ½inches, now world-wide. One writer thought it dated from the last century only while another attributed it to the Romans. But evidently it is much older still. At Syracuse I selected some clear wheel tracks of the 4th century BC and found them to be exactly 4 feet 8½ inches between the inner edges of the iron tyres. Here at Agrigento I have photographed a measuring rod in position; the print shows the ends quite exactly over the inner edges of the Greek tyres of the 5th century BC. An old disused stone quarry at Viterbo also shows clear wheel tracks precisely 4 feet 8 ½ inches, inside measurement of iron tyres'.

[2] Henry Robert Hardcastle's name also shares the face of the tombstone, without dates. He is not, in fact, buried there.

express approval of Marconi.

Things were changing in Mussolini's Italy as the heavy hand of fascism made itself felt even more. The Ministry of Education in Rome, while gratefully accepting his money with one hand, sometimes slapped him in the face with the other. An interoffice memorandum out of Rome reiterated that 'with regard to the excavations financed by Captain Hardcastle in Agrigento, I must inform you that the said excavations, although executed with the funding of a private individual, must, in accordance with the law, figure as having been carried out by the State.' The public, in other words, was not to be reminded overtly that an Englishman had held the purse strings. Alexander did not record his feelings about this. He was anonymously accused of hoarding Valley treasures at home or maybe even exporting them. To quash the rumours, Orsi ordered Pirro Marconi to go in person to check. 'I was able to look throughout Capt. H.'s house and I can assure you that he is not housing a museum there, save some little mass-produced items and the antifix from the Temple of Herakles for which he had … permission and which he had already offered to give back to me. I also know that he has steadfastly refused to buy ancient objects offered to him by the farmers and the antiquarians.' Still, the whispers and slurs continued. One of Hardcastle's letters of late 1926 to Orsi in Syracuse concerning proposed works on the Temple of Vulcan was translated into Italian for easier reading. The letter bore an anonymous gibe, added at the foot of the page: 'May God send us lots more of these nice art lovers who have no ulterior motives, *even if they are foreigners!*'.

Word had it that behind the scenes a number of Girgenti's noteworthies had been instructed to keep a watchful eye on the two brothers and report to the local *Podestà*[3] Ignazio Altieri any suspect movements at or around the Villa Aurea. Anything that might have revealed the brothers as spies, maybe? And, incidentally, those marble tablets affixed to a handful of Hardcastle's costly repairs struck some as a provocation, a red rag to the bull. One of those irritated by the plaques was Antonino Arancio. Born in Girgenti and sixteen years younger than the Englishman, Arancio had not had the privileged upbringing of the foreigner. He had not gone beyond elementary school and had had to take a modest bank clerking job after The Great War. Nonetheless, fascinated by Greek mythology and archaeology to the point of naming his children Ulysses, Penelope and Esseneto after an ancient Greek athlete, he taught himself everything he could about it and began guiding tourists around the Valley. He earned their favour, also, as 'he quoted Homer's rolling verses in his musical tones'. He became proficient enough to be appointed 'sub-official' custodian to the Valley, taking just as proprietary an interest as Hardcastle. Like low-rung bureaucrats worldwide, Arancio enjoyed wielding his baton zealously over his turf, ready to do battle over the fine print. Writing to Marconi, he took issue with Leo Trippi, the owner of the Grand Hôtel Des Temples for

---

[3] By 1926, local self-government was abolished; in February the new law affected all towns with a population of up to 5000. By early September, it was extended to *all* towns. The fascist regime replaced Italy's mayors with centrally-nominated *podestà*.

digging on the grounds of his establishment: 'I'd advise him to await your arrival to set out a <u>proper</u> archaeological dig rather than doing as he does, flitting here and there.' But he reserved his real firepower for Hardcastle. As 1926 came to a close, no longer able to contain suppressed resentment of the Villa Aurea occupants, he took up his pen and wrote a tattletaling letter to Orsi in Syracuse. People were *always* dumping their personal spites on either Orsi's or Marconi's lap!

> Wishing to show particular courtesy to the foreigner Capt. Alex Hardcastle, who has made himself useful in carrying out works to this archaeological site, I have refrained from denouncing him to the authorities for having placed … marble tablets with dedications which I transcribe herewith. But to fulfil my holy duty, I feel compelled to report this to your Office in order for steps to be taken. The tablets are affixed in the Temple of Demeter, on the north wall of the rock, standing about two meters off the ground [as well as at another temple]. I await whatever orders you may wish to give me [concerning this matter].
>
> I remain most respectfully yours.<br>The Subordinate Custodian,<br>Antonino Arancio

Orsi gently finessed the matter with a velvety rebuke: 'may I allow myself to urge you not to put up plaques [without the clearance] … of this superintendency, inasmuch as several improprieties of this nature have been noted.' At this stage, only two such tablets had gone up. But they profoundly antagonised some.

The mood had definitely changed and there would be further unpleasantness down the road. Intrigued by George Dennis's descriptions of Etruscan settlements in Etruria, Alick and Harry went out exploring one early summer day of 1930 around the remains of Roselle, five miles to the north of Grosseto. Alarmed by the sight of two pale tall foreigners in the middle of nowhere, the police arrested them on suspicion of spying and brought them into their local precinct. And there they remained until the British Consulate came to the rescue. Hardcastle reacted just as a Victorian-age military man always did: he rolled up his sleeves and got on with life.

# –19–

The Greek perimeter walls, the eight august columns of Herakles, the quest for a theatre, the uncovering of the Demeter site were the sizeable, eye-catching accomplishments of these last five years. They had made the headlines not only in Sicily, but also abroad. They had boosted the number of visitors. But remarkably, they were *not* all that was going on. Hardcastle was anxious – almost feverish! – to keep the momentum up. Slackening, he reckoned, would be fatal. Slow-footing was not one of his traits. 'I have received Doctor Marconi's report on the 1925 excavations and I hope soon to have a still greater report on the *scavi di 1926*', he commented.

The wherewithal to pay for all this remains an enigma. The settlement from his father was handsome and money went a very long way in Sicily. The rate of exchange had been very generous to him at the outset; he kept his accounts with the Banca Commerciale Italiana in Palermo. The mystery arises, however, when the Lira was revalued in 1927 and his sterling took a pummelling over the exchange counter: how did he continue to sustain the same financial outgoings, with fewer Lire in his pocket? Perhaps substantial funds had been transferred all in one go at the very beginning, when he first arrived in Sicily and the exchange tilted in his favour. Surviving correspondence, however, does not support this. Over the years, Hardcastle's correspondence refers to 'if things [excavations] go well, I shall be happy to add to the ... offer', 'at present, I cannot do more', 'I've just had word about my funds in London and it seems that for (only) one year, I will be unable to offer more ... .' In other words, he was transferring his sterling a bit at a time, having to pace himself and learn to live with the slipping value of his English money. Nonetheless, it did not seem to dent his uncurbable drive: 'the *scavi agrigentini*', he noted, 'are growing every year'.

There was the area of another temple to clear, and the north wall of the cella of the Temple of Herakles ('this work would clear the whole floor of the cella and give a better vision of the whole temple').

As Christmas 1926 neared, he learned that the owner of the land where the Temple of Hephaistos (Vulcan) was located agreed to an expropriation '... nobody has excavated this temple of which the stylobate and 2 columns at least remain (+ perhaps much more below ground). It is not difficult or expensive.'

Orsi, who was never short of letters from the Villa Aurea, soon received a follow-up to Hardcastle's musings about Hephaistos:

> I have instructed my banker to send you Lire 50,000 on the 1$^{st}$ of January – the

excavation of the necropolis (cemetery) will be interesting but I hope you will spend the larger part of the funds on the Temples – either to find another telemon or to clear the site of 'Vulcano' or to restore the cella of 'Eracle'.

He explained pedantically to Orsi why he thought this was most important:

(a) There are already thousands of vases, but only very few Temples
(b) The vases are put into Museums where only <u>students</u> see them, but the temples remain for ever

These three projects would 'be a magnificent programme for 1927', he thought.

The ever faithful Harry, meanwhile, filled his days tending as well as he could to the domestic details of the Villa Aurea for his busy brother and passed time walking the hills, writing letters and occasionally, in his naïveté, getting into trouble. Overeating pork fat, he took to bed with bad stomach aches. He got himself fleeced by restaurant waiters in Palermo on visits to the Anglican Church there. His cherished newspapers from England somehow were often going astray.

## –20–

Like many Englishmen of his generation, Hardcastle took a lively interest in gardening and landscaping. Embellishing his own terrace and compound grounds became a point of pride and a way of removing himself momentarily from the sometimes stifling milieu of archaeology. If not at 38 Eaton Square, then certainly at Moor House in Oxted, he would have known and drawn inspiration from his parents' luxuriant grounds. He was not, of course, in the league of some English settlers in Italy both before and after his time and nor did he want to be. There were people such as Sir Thomas Hanbury who over forty years on his private grounds at La Mortola in Liguria, just by the French border, had amassed some five thousand exotic plant species in a heady botanic cocktail throughout the late 1860s–1870s. The Director of Kew Gardens said of it in 1893 that 'in point of richness … [it] has no rival amongst the private collections of living plants in the world'. Or Scotland's Captain Neil MacEacharn who in the 1930s shaped the forty-nine-acre gardens of his Villa Taranto on a promontory of Lake Maggiore, endowing this magnificent property with rare plants from around the world. Those were men who, with their keen head gardeners and willing helpers, were almost professionally engaged in swaps with far-flung botanists and prelates for cuttings and seeds from other climes.

Nonetheless, there were trees and plants that Hardcastle probably recalled from his Asian and African days which would thrive in the equally warm temperatures of Sicily; he did not hesitate to order samples up from contacts abroad. Probably turning to acquaintances from South Africa, he imported three jacaranda trees, with their thick mass of lilac-blue trumpet-shaped blossoms. Their bold splash of colour made a cheerful contrast to his sun-bleached slopes in the Valley. One was planted on the grounds of the Villa Aurea. One was a gift to the Miceli family who ran the local pharmacy and owned a grand home, the Villa Ofelia, near to his in the valley. The third is unaccounted for or quite possibly did not acclimatise.

Alick proudly sent one photograph back to the family captioned 'Terrace of the Villa Aurea with flowering aloes and asphodels on left of sun-dial'. Drought-tolerant aloes with their orange droplet-like flowers and the white-petalled asphodels were ideal for the busy bachelor. They were low-maintenance plants. To his brother Alfred's widow, Theresa he confided 'I have not much leisure, as I have to run 2 houses and gardens'. From Viterbo on another occasion he sent her a view of the Villa Palanzana saying 'this is the old Etruscan ravine (200 feet deep) with our wild garden along the top of it & our mountain beyond'.

At the Grand Hôtel des Temples up the hill from the Villa Aurea, the Swiss proprietor-manager Leo Trippi tended the most resplendent garden of all Girgenti. Set out at the foot of the grand terrace were winding grass and pebbled pathways, stately conifers and palms and formal flower beds literally exploding in colour. The famed English-born American archaeologist David Randall-MacIver and his wife Joanna stayed there twice, the latter visit in March 1930 while he was busy with Alick researching his book '*Greek Cities in Italy and Sicily*'. In one letter back home, Joanna wrote glowingly of the garden '... stocks of every hue, superb cinerarias, calla lilies, freesia, anemones, snapdragons ... masses of flowers in a garden thick with bloom ...'. Another visitor admired the 'twenty different tropical fruit trees' and the 'over 100 varieties of cactus'. No one left Trippi's Eden indifferent to what they had seen.

*Grand Hôtel des Temples, Agrigento.*

But greenery was something meant for the populace as well and not just Alexander's own private quarters. Trees could provide shade from the merciless sun and they could set off to advantage the ancient sites. They could provide harmless fodder for those goats who otherwise would rampage over the relics. And they would certainly embellish and add dignity to the growing network of public roads.

It is not such a paradox as it might at first seem that on one hand he spent much energy on ridding both the Valley and Ferento of vegetation while on the other, replanting with equal gusto. The straggly and unsightly weeds that had taken over so much *had* to go; they strangled everything in their midst and were more of an eyesore than anything else. Once cleared, there was more room to plant serious things which would enhance the general beauty of the landscape. By the summer of 1926, he was pleading for the 'foresting' of Girgenti, 'particularly along the roads'. When those pleas momentarily fell on deaf ears, he renewed the barrage. Marconi was usually his first port of call, even though urban matters were of no concern to him. He wrote to the *podestà*, the prefect, Sinatra or anyone else within earshot! 'I am desirous to promote reforestation here in Girgenti and especially to plant pines, cypresses and broom near the Agrigentan antiquities. I'd like to create a little wooded area above the Temple of Demeter and protect it completely against the goats. [Then I'd like] to plant around San Nicolò and by the approaches to the temples, such plants as you deem appropriate and all robustly protected against the goats.' He added a little later that 'I'd like to plant pines and other trees along the the Rupe Atenea, the Athenian Rock … and also some eucalyptus beneath the chapels of the Cemetery and also by the Bonamorone fountain'. Many of the rows of trees that finally went in due to his prodding were a feast to the eyes of the increasing stream of visitors. And many of them still work their magic today. Lastly, he gave thought, too, to beautifying the spot where he would ultimately rest, putting in young cypresses which grew to stately dimensions. His friend Sinatra reckoned that, in all, Hardcastle spent 15,000 Lire of yesterday's money on plantings alone. His public spirit did not end there, however. He had donated to advantage one toilet for the Hotel Belvedere and he now financed two more for the townsfolk elsewhere in town.

Perhaps he was aware of his countryman Leonard Hawksley who in those same years was travelling up and down Italy, waging a personal battle against cruelty to animals. Hawksley intervened whenever he caught sight of horses being beaten, birds incarcerated in unusually small cages, dogs being maltreated. The Whitakers in Palermo had supported Hawksley's good works and now Hardcastle took inspiration from his compatriot's benevolence. He witnessed daily the spectacle of donkeys and mules climbing the steep paths of the Valley, hauling heavy water jugs and supplies to the archaeological site but never given water themselves. At his expense, pipes were run down from Agrigento. Fountains and troughs were built. People *and* animals could now quench their thirst.

He railed when the beauty was marred: 25 electricity poles and billboards *had* to be removed, he commanded. The mere sight of a recently-installed electricity box near the temples 'gives me a bad stomach ache'. He got that painted over hastily. And then he sprang into action when news got out that the city fathers were contemplating an extension of the railroad line … right to the front entrance into the temple grounds. 'It is doubly absurd – it costs too much and foreigners without luggage far prefer approaching the site by carriage.' The prospect of a rail station would have spelled the definitive destruction of the Valley. A first length of the tunnel had been bored through the hillside in the direction of the valley, then halted. No further digging took place and the project was quietly shelved.

'I absolutely wish to see a national museum here', he boomed before long. What existed already was in a truly woeful state. Just opposite the town hall, the roof of the civic museum building leaked, walls were mouldy, windows broken. The exhibition space was cramped and part of the collection had to be housed in a deconsecrated church elsewhere in town. In short, it in no way was a showcase to present to visitors. He paid 25,000 to repair the building, turning it into an airy, dignified exhibition space.

## –21–

For years, both before and after Hardcastle's death, whispers circulated about Alexander Hardcastle's personal persuasions. Sicily had lured its share of homosexual visitors. The name Baron Wilhelm von Glœden is probably deep below memory's general dust heap today. But once that name alone was code word for the homosexual coterie that gravitated around Taormina, to the east of Agrigento, throughout the latter half of the 1800s and well into the first half of the 1900s.

Taormina has been a cultural draw for at least 250 years, ever since the first important restoration to the Greek theatre there. Accommodation for early visitors was reckoned, however, to be 'sordide, crasseuse, noirâtre et nauséabonde'. Gradually standards improved and people flocked in from Paris, London and plenty of points in Germany, comforted by better lodgings. In addition to the antiquities, visitors started arriving for other attractions: the picturesque scenery, the seaside, a place to recover from tuberculosis and a spot of easy sexual transgression. That was tolerated if not endorsed.

At first, the hotel registers tilted towards German travellers, followed by the English. Later, the balance reversed. Just before World War I, these foreigners were not just *visiting* Taormina, however. Families were *settling* there, acquiring houses or land and building themselves sun-drenched, balustraded villas. By the early 1920s, their numbers had swollen sufficiently to band together in building an Anglican Church. Some 35 foreign families called Taormina home. Meanwhile, a parallel community of writers and artists was also building in size. Their personal inclinations, though, were of another nature. Some were simply visitors. Others settled. They included Karl von Stempel, Roger Peyrefitte, Oscar Wilde, Jean Cocteau, Robert Kitson. Luxury trains stuffed with 'la crème de la crème of European pederasty' – as one person put it – chugged southwards to join the homosexual community.

They all had been preceded by the son of a German baron, Wilhelm von Glœden, who came to Sicily in the 1870s to recuperate from tuberculosis in the warm, dry climate of the island's eastern shores. He became known for his largesse towards the townsfolk whom he aided generously in all manner, much in the same spirit as Hardcastle. When he heard of neediness, he offered work for the indigent. He provided dowries for young brides about to start off married life. Von Glœden soon took up photography as a hobby. Because of his unapologetic sexual leanings, though, he rapidly became notorious for one particular sort of image. Handsome local boys were recruited to pose – quite often in the nude – for his classical *tableaux vivants* photographed amongst the antiquities. Given the dire poverty and the eagerness to keep financially above the water, the *taorminesi* held their tongues and looked the other way as they sent their sons up the hill to stand in *en dishabille* before von Glœden's camera.

To have in any way bunched Hardcastle with this community, however, was wholly unwarranted. Von Glœden openly acknowledged the young men sharing his quarters, while there is not a single shred of evidence of young male companions at the Villa Aurea. Such comings and goings would have been immediately spotted and openly commented upon in a rural place like Girgenti. In all correspondence with male associates over the thirteen years spent in Italy, it unfailingly was of a professional nature. Never is there even a remote hint of sexual intimacy. He showed compassionate concern, just as much as the next person, towards friends and colleagues whether male or female. He was solicitous towards Marconi when the latter fell ill with winter flu, recommending appropriate medicine. 'I am sorry to hear that you have caught cold. I always take 15 cg. of aspirin together with 15 cg. of quinine every four hours – the results are miraculous! I am not only a distinguished archaeologist, but also a doctor!' And, when Marconi had improved, 'I hope you have regained your appetite', he wrote. He wished the young archaeologist well for his holidays: 'I hope that you'll now go off to the sea or to the mountains with your family and without any books!' and afterwards, 'I hope you have returned to Palermo after pleasant holidays in the Trentino amidst the Dolomites, the most beautiful place in the world.'

Warmth and friendliness towards his men friends was not, though, to be construed as homosexuality. He certainly was not averse to the fair sex if they were easy on the eye; invariably, though, it was the stout and sturdy-shod sort that made it to his doorstep (in a letter to Marconi enclosing a clipping from The Times, he explained that the piece he had written was unsigned 'because otherwise I'd have no peace. Everyone seems to come to the Villa Aurea, from our King's personal physician to lady journalists – *stile severo!*').

Burgeoning Victorian and Edwardian families were legendary for the number of offspring who *didn't* walk up the aisle. Indeed, only two of Alick's seven siblings wed. And that was the pattern for many. In 1901 when Alexander had reached the very marriageable age of 29, just over 49% of the male population of England and Wales between the ages of 21 and 65 were unwed. It was a trend reflected in the United States as well. Writing of similar patterns in 'The Age of the Bachelor', Howard Chudacoff notes of the phenomenon in America that 'the number and proportion of unmarried men in urban communities increased markedly in the last third of the nineteenth century and a large number of the older, more financially secure bachelors lived with one or more parents'. Alexander's years in the military, also, certainly had not afforded him the opportunity to find and court a prospective bride. The barracks of Singapore and the war front in South Africa had not been optimum hunting grounds for matrimony. And the Hardcastles, as we have been reminded, were a clan of loners in life, each with strong strains of independence.

Alexander had already suffered two mental breakdowns before arriving in Sicily and it is not unreasonable to suppose that he feared inflicting a third bout on an unprepared wife. The previous two incidences had marked his mother's life: he had seen that with his own eyes. He would not have wished Maria Sophia's sorrow on a wife as well. Bachelorhood forced on him by circumstance did not make him a soul mate of von Glœden. Alexander Hardcastle was not then a homosexual. Nor was he ever.

# -22-

Mussolini's chosen man in Agrigento,[1] Podestà Ignazio Altieri, woke up and dressed as usual one warm morning in the late spring of 1928. Francesco Sinatra came to join him and together the two men headed down the hill. All the delays were now behind them, delays caused by indecision over which decoration to confer, by the required approval of the British Government and by Hardcastle's regular long summer absences from Agrigento. Even Orsi had written restlessly to Sinatra from Syracuse on October 29, 1927: had Altieri actually received the medal for safekeeping and when on earth was Hardcastle getting back to Agrigento from the north? The months had tumbled by, but now a date had been set and the formalities could go forward. They had to hurry, however, because Alick really wished to be off, back to the Villa Palanzana. Summer was on the doorstep and Sicily was getting hot.

The two men quickened their pace, mindful of Hardcastle's English love of punctuality. Altieri was carrying a small red rectangular box, the lid of which bore an embossed gold crown and the stylised letters 'V' and 'E', for Vittorio Emanuele. The King of Italy. The box and its contents came from the noted Rome jeweller, O. Cravanzola, the appointed royal supplier of official decorations and craftsman of fine medals and trophy cups. But it was what was inside the little red box that counted, as the two men made their way through the stone portal into the Villa Aurea grounds.

The mission that morning in the tiled sitting room of the Villa was to slip the red and white ribbon around Alexander's neck. Orsi assigned Sinatra, as honorary archaeological inspector at Agrigento, to conduct the ceremony. Nearby, Harry watched proudly, attentively as his older brother dipped slightly for Sinatra's hands to reach over his head. From the ribbon hung the enamelled decoration of the Order of the Crown of Italy. The medal itself bore four fan-shaped white 'petals' set on a red background. In the very centre was a small crown, an eagle and a white cross.

Mention had been made earlier of conferring the order of Saints Maurizio and Lazzaro. On the recommendation of the Italian State, however, the king was 'pleased to bestow the Cross of *Commendatore* of the Order of the Crown of Italy [as it was then called] on the British subject Captain Alessandro Hardcastle whose very deserving merits are known'. The degree of commendatore ranked third highest and was rarely awarded to foreigners and thus all the more precious to Hardcastle as he stood there, surrounded by

---

[1] In 1927, the government decreed name changes for a number of towns, rendering them more Italian or Roman. Thus 'beginning in the new financial year, starting July 1', Girgenti became Agrigento, while Castrogiovanni was re-minted Enna and Terranova, once again, became Gela.

a coterie of close friends for the simple ceremony. Glasses were lifted afterwards and toasts made to the health of the Englishman. From that day forward, he proudly used his new Italian title and even had it carved in advance on his tombstone. Generally unfamiliar with honorifics, everyday Italians equated the Italian honour with the English title of 'Sir' and so began, erroneously, the habit of calling him 'Sir Hardcastle'. In point of fact, Hardcastle's achievements were *never* fully broadcast in his homeland, his name was *never* put forward and King George V *did not* knight him. But that in no way diminished his feelings of pride. Indeed, he probably felt more privileged being an Italian *commendatore*. It was something special, something apart.

The congratulations poured in and he basked in the accolades, mustering moments of faint modesty. 'I prefer continuing my work for Italy without any official fuss', he said to one. 'The honour is almost too much, but I hope to have the pleasure of collaborating on behalf of Agrigento for many years to come', was the comment to another. And in reply to warm congratulations from someone else, he wrote, 'the decoration seems like too high an honour ... unless you count the building of two public lavatories, my masterpiece!'

By then, Hardcastle was moved enough to make a fraternal gesture towards his own country which had permitted him to receive this decoration. It was time to donate something to one of the grandest repositories of antiquities of them all, The British Museum in London. The excavation campaign of 1927 had unearthed a particularly rich trove of fragments of terracotta sculpture near the Villa Aurea, all of which lay languishing, undisplayed, on a storage shelf at the Agrigento museum. Reckoning that replication of some of them would stir up the least commotion, he sought and received permission from Marconi to send a selection of eighteen pieces off to Syracuse to be professionally copied. Plaster moulds would be sent to England of such sculptured themes as a Gorgon clasping snakes, a man carrying a goat, three seated women, a squatting ape, a woman astride a cockerel. In Syracuse, the 18 pieces lingered for another year and the beleaguered Marconi reached for his pen to referee complaints: 'I have been under continual pressure from the authorities of Agrigento', he wrote in the summer of 1929 to the Superintendency at Syracuse, 'to have [the loaned material] returned. I would be grateful to you (having signed off the authorization for these objects in 1928 and thus having personally to answer to the authorities of Agrigento), if upon [completion of the work] you would return the material, freeing me of the continual pestering to which I am now subjected!' It wasn't, however, until six months later that Syracuse informed the British Museum that the shipment had departed. The prim letters from Syracuse counselled London 'to please thank the donor' and 'to please confirm the safe arrival of the crate'.[2] London duly complied. (The items are today stored in the

---

[2] Alexander expressed hope that the heads of two gigantic telemons (the column-like supports in the form of a man, the male equivalent of a caryatid) from the Temple of Zeus could also be replicated and sent to the British Museum. Casts of these gracefully sculpted heads with their stylised wavy coifs, however, were not made and London did not receive them.

repository of the Museum) Interestingly, the inventory of the Department of Greek and Roman Antiquities at the British Museum today reveals a further Hardcastle donation as well, in 1957, of three small pieces of pottery. Alick by then had been dead for 24 years. It was a gift from Felicité and she was turning over a late Hellenistic jug and two Attic-period open vessels, in all likelihood inherited from one of her deceased Hardcastle relatives. Alick had probably been given the items by a farmer and quietly sent them on to a member of his family, perhaps Theresa. It was further evidence that not all ties with his siblings had been irreparably severed.

Hardcastle's decoration had come shortly after another pleasing event. The Ministry of Education mounted a gracious marble plaque on the entrance wall of the Theatre of Ferento in warm tribute to Hardcastle's generosity and to the man who had inspired him, George Dennis. Quite possibly, Hardcastle made a quick, off-season dash north for the unveiling ceremony. All the palaver over new bricks versus old bricks was now behind him and the two brothers were able to look up and read the words:

**LA R. SOPRINTENDENZA ALLE ANTICHITA' DI ROMA
COMPLETO SCAVI E RESTAURI DEL TEATRO DI FERENTO
CON DANARO OFFERTO DAL CAPITANO AL. HARDCASTLE
CHE VOLLE IN TAL MODO ONORARE
IL NOBILE SUO CONNAZIONALE G. DENNIS
ILLUSTRATORE SAPIENTE DELLA ANTICA ETRURIA
ANNO MCMXXVII**[3]

Alick dropped a short note to Paribeni in Rome 'I showed … the marble tablet to a very old friend of George Dennis and it gave great pleasure'.

Viterbo beckoned. Before leaving, Hardcastle sat down at his desk to draw a diagram, as he did every year, of the rooms of the Villa Aurea, fastidiously noting the positioning of all his household belongings. (None of these 'maps' survive, unfortunately.) On his autumn return, he would check that everything was exactly as he left it months earlier. As a small boy, Calogero Miceli, remembered being escorted around the house with the caretaker one summer and being admonished: 'don't touch a thing! *L'inglese* knows exactly where everything is and I'll get in trouble if things aren't where he left them.' With that, Alick and Harry packed their bags and headed north.

There was no shortage of other projects to keep him busy, now that the 'Ferento campaign' had wound down. Etruscan remains thickly dotted the Etrurian landscape around Viterbo. An excursion the summer before with Costantino Zei to Castel d'Asso west of Viterbo, piqued his curiosity about an Etruscan necropolis. If they could clear away the undergrowth, perhaps they would discover a Roman-Etruscan bi-lingual inscription on one of the tombs. It seemed like a meaty challenge at the very least.

---

[3] Trans: The Superintendency of Antiquities in Rome. Completion of excavations and restorations to the Theatre of Ferento with money donated by Captain Al. Hardcastle who in this manner wished to honour his noble countryman George Dennis, learned writer about ancient Etruria.

## Chapter 22

'Luckily, inscriptions have no intrinsic value', he told himself reassuringly, 'so they probably haven't all been destroyed.' But the challenge went further than simple poring over graveyard inscriptions. 'Studying isn't enough; you've really got to sweat', he told a friend.

That summer the 393-foot long *dromos* or corridor leading into an Etruscan crematorium was brought to light at Castel d'Asso. His mind wandered. After Castel d'Asso, why not Sutri or Bolsena? In point of fact, Alick mobilized work teams that fanned out around to no fewer than *five* Etruscan sites circling Viterbo and had them clear detritus, shore up crumbling walls, cut access paths, record details, sketch remains, study the remaining structures of crematoria, run protective barbed wire around the perimeters of the sites. And over and over, he repeated his mantra to anyone who would listen: 'my desire is to make these splendid … remains more accessible to visitors, and thus to awaken interest for <u>further</u> excavations.' Others, he reckoned, would be inspired to pick up the baton.

Work, meanwhile, was no less *movimentato* in Sicily over those two years, 1927 and 1928. He spelled out an ever-expanding 'wish list' on many occasions, rattling off possible projects. 'We've got to study further those large sculptured pieces near the Greek aqueduct', 'the steps to the Temple of Æsculapius[4] must be made safe, belted in with a metal band and I'd like to excavate the Temple of Ephestus', 'some eucalyptus trees need to be planted beneath the cemetery chapels and near the Bonamorone fountain.'

That local museum had been little more than a woefully damp and mouldy repository with a leaking roof just opposite the town hall. It was a sad state of affairs and as he pointed out to Paolo Orsi quite reasonably, 'it is almost pointless to be excavating if we don't have a worthy and commodious museum!' That, too, it will be remembered was given a new lease of life, re-roofed, painted and fitted up with new display cases and lighting.

A stretch of Roman mosaic paving had been discovered and restored. Then he fixed his sites on the ruins of the Temple of Vulcan dedicated to the god of fire, on the extreme western side of the Valley complex. Two Doric columns were all that still stood upright, resting on the remains of the stone foundation: 'I would like to pay <u>all</u> of the Vulcan excavation costs', he wrote to Marconi.

---

[4] Of which part of the walls standing between the Tomb of Theron and the confluence of the city's two rivers still survived.

# -23-

All along, Hardcastle had been a superb organizer. He knew how to draw up a list of achievable goals, to set deadlines, how to nudge campaigns firmly along through the official channels and, like a troika driver, how to hold together the straggly, disparate strands straining in different directions, on through to completion. Seemingly, there was even time left over for *other* pastimes. An assiduous reader of *The Times*, he shot off opinions and had his say in their 'Letters Column' regularly, when piqued by a topic. He reported the passage of migrating cranes from Africa, applauded the idea of returning the British Museum's caryatids to Athens, noted the inequities of import duties, praised fascist Italy's reduction of salaries and retail prices and attacked the repugnant proposals of London's eugenics advocates to sterilise the feeble-minded. He followed world events just as attentively as the digs close to his home.

To use a modern term, he was a fine micromanager over all that interested him. So much so that it was beginning to blind him to his other failings. If he was good at getting workers to shovel and masons to mend ancient structures, increasingly, he did not see the very few first hints of cracks that needed attention in his very own makeup. The fissures were imperceptible, but they were beginning. The manic drive to spend on excavations should have sounded the first alarm bells as it went on unabated, much like the urge that propels addicted gamblers to the gaming table. He was never altogether sure where the money would come from. But that did not seem to hold back his spending ways.

Such wild abandon with the purse, meanwhile, had not touched his family back in England. Maria Sophia was approaching her 90$^{th}$ year and still resided at Oxted. There were still faithful retainers to look after her in the inevitable decline, but remarkably for those days, none of her surviving children troubled to move nearby. Up in Northumberland near the Scottish border, Frances had chosen the farthest distance in the country from Oxted at which to reside. Beautiful Beatrice, 'who could live with no one', seemed in perpetual motion, flitting from one address to another. Eleanor was at Farnham, Mira in Hindhead, John at Sidcup. Joseph Alfred's widow Theresa made Burley her home with her daughter Felicité down in the New Forest. There were visits to their mother's large, rambling Moor House, checking in on her as she grew ever frailer but none of them actually moved in to keep vigil. All came, except the two sons in Sicily. When she finally did slip away on a frosty Tuesday morning, January 8, 1929, she had not seen this pair for eight years. In the small cortège following her coffin into the graveyard adjoining the local church were all her surviving children, save two, to see her to her final resting place beside her husband.

## Chapter 23

*The Moor House home of Henry and Maria Sophia Hardcastle, Oxted, from 1905.
The photograph was taken in the 1960s when the building served as a local school.
(Courtesy of John Lea)*

Whatever lingering rancours there might have been between Alexander and his mother, they had to have haunted him in his remaining 41 months of life, and indeed, even coloured his inner thoughts, however well he may have concealed them to the outside world. As always, there was plenty to distract him. The journal *Antiquity* was reporting further activity in the Valley: a circular opening of stone blocks found near the Temple of the Dioscuri (Castor and Pollux) proved to be the *bothros* of an altar, the sacred vent in the ground through which the faithful communed with the gods. Three archaic altars were uncovered and pottery in abundance. Unquestionably, Alick was in the full swim of it.

Maria Sophia Hardcastle's death brought no further inheritance to him. Her remaining estate consisted in just over £900 pounds and she left this to Mira Francisca and to Eleanor Constance as well as various coveted personal effects: a diamond ring, a gold locket with a portrait of Maria Sophia's father, various silver teapots, other pieces of jewellery. In his letters to Marconi scarcely a fortnight after his mother's death, Alexander revealed no hint of sadness and made no mention of her passing. He did, however, think to report on the welfare of his brother. The winter weather in Agrigento was gloomy – 'yesterday cold and rainy' – and Harry was in bed nursing a cold, meaning that Alick, too, was 'house-bound, obliged to tend to his [sibling's] needs'. Dispensing money for the completion of work on the Temple of Hephaistos (Vulcan) and for studying the remains of a recently discovered archaic altar was insistently on his mind. But now the sums were starting to get smaller. One thousand here, one thousand there. Sometimes, there was 'good news from London', enabling him to spend more. But increasingly, he had to be careful. 'I've sold off another car, so I can send off another cheque for L1000', he wrote Marconi.

Then, on October 24, 1929, disaster struck, 4500 miles from Agrigento. A catastrophe with a devastating ripple effect that affected him, together with millions of others. 'I don't think it will be possible for me this winter to fund excavations', he informed the authorities in Palermo, 'because of the "stock market crash" in New York and London. It is <u>very serious!</u> I will have to limit myself to small things.' Yet, in virtually the same breath, he showed his increasing disconnect with reality by vowing to help Giovanni Ziretta cover the costs of new glass display cases and shelving at the Civic Museum, which Ziretta directed, contributing to the costs of making casts of the heads of the gigantic telamons that once supported the Zeus temple portals, up-righting a fallen column by the Temple of Demeter, cleaning up around the Temple of Zeus and so on.

It didn't end there. Even before the stock market crash, he was losing his firm grip not only on his pocket book, but also his grip on patience and a calm demeanour. Learning that one worksite foreman had taken off in the height of the summer heat from Viterbo for a deserved vacation break, he thundered his disapproval, indignant over the man's brief absence. Rest was almost an unfamiliar term to him and, inflexibly, he rarely could understand others needing a respite. The imperious behaviour got worse. After four very smooth summers working harmoniously with Costantino Zei around the province of Viterbo, relations turned decidedly sour. The two men had worked side by side all that time, driving the hilly countryside to sites of interest to Alexander. But then Zei was pushed just one step too far. He sat down in his room at the Albergo dell'Angelo in Viterbo one mid-April evening of 1929 and poured out his rage in a letter to Roberto Paribeni in Rome. Writing in his small tight script, he catalogued his grievances:

> Hardcastle asked me to carry out research that required numerous trips out of town, he asked me to oversee excavations, to write up reports and send him newspaper clippings, to write various people, to meet with local authorities and others, etc etc. and all of this went on for two years without so much as a word about any sort of payment other than the occasional reimbursement for ongoing expenses, such as he deemed acceptable. This February, he wished me to deal with the sale of one of his cars, stipulating that he expected it to fetch 14,000 Lire. I was unable to get more than 11,000 and even that was a good deal. In a letter from Girgenti [sic], he wrote that he accepted that sum adding that because of the difference of 3000 Lire he saw no need to pay me a fee as the go-between. It was as if he was implying that if I wanted any recompense, I should seek it from the new buyers or that I had done some sort of deal with them behind his back. Following this, I decided to have done with him, given his rude behaviour, in spite of him being English. I have never asked him for money in payment for all my work. I simply sent him a breakdown of what I had done and left

it to his conscience to do as he saw fit. He replied that rather than a professional's bill he would have preferred 'a friendly settlement'. One would have thought with that, that he conceded that something was due. But it was not to be. In a series of letters, postcards and telegrams that followed, he refused any settlement whatsoever, heaping on me the most vulgar of insults to which I replied as calmly as I could. And today I read in a report that he sent to you yet further insults not only about me but also others who honour me with their friendship. In fact, he even says that he fears coming to Viterbo because of possible reprisals to him by either me or my friends. In essence, he seems to be accusing me of being a brigand chief! … In light of the unspeakable behaviour of this Englishman I am considering going to law. I would be grateful for your views and whether you feel I should resign from my role as president of the Monument Conservation Commission for the Province of Viterbo.

In a letter written five months later, Hardcastle made a detached passing reference to this affair: 'Here in Viterbo, after six months of threats and insults, I broke with Professor Zei (who wants to extract money from a foreigner) and I now deal with Professor Romanelli … .'

These were among the first ominous signs of his unmooring.

# -24-

Early on at Girgenti, Alick not only knew that he wanted to be buried there, but also that he wanted to bequeath his most prized possession, the Villa Aurea, to the Italian State. By the end of 1924, he had approached the British Consulate at Palermo for legal advice and was guided to a local lawyer. He was 52 and felt the time had come to put shape to his wishes in writing. The will was drawn up and dated January 8, 1926, the same year that Girgenti gave him a free plot at the Bonamorone Cemetery. In the will, he set out his dream: on his death, the Villa Aurea would become a centre for artists and academics of all nations. Only six university graduates at a time would be accommodated. It would be free and the stay would be restricted to one month, during which time approved projects had to be pursued, much in the spirit of a fellowship program today. Further, money would be left to cover upkeep and staffing costs – expenses that the perennially-strapped Ministry of Education could ill afford. The remainder of his estate would be available for excavations. Of Greek, not Roman, sites, he stressed. He clearly assumed in 1926 that the money to do all of this would be available from investments in Britain. Of his family, only Henry Robert was to receive anything, namely personal effects and funds to cover funeral costs. No provisions for his other brother and sisters were made.

The centre would bear his name, keeping alive his memory. 'I am confident', he told Sinatra, 'that in the hands [of the State] … the Villa Aurea will never be invaded by the public, nor will it be desecrated by the ignorant.' Rome once again was happy to accept the proposed gift and only asked that he verify that the inheritance laws of his birthplace would allow this; these formalities were satisfied accordingly.[1] His home would belong to Italy upon his death.

By late in 1932, however, matters had already taken a tragic turn for many. The 1929 stock market crash had seen many banks fail; a major recession soon followed. The United Kingdom left the gold standard and devalued the pound. By 1933, unemployment would climb to 25% of the work force. It was simply a question of time before, domino-style, Alexander's bank in London, too, would be swept into the vortex of economic and social chaos and succumb, together with his investments. Details of neither his English bank nor his financial portfolio survive, other than one early, vague reference to Alexander's interests in the rubber industry. Nonetheless, it is clear that the axe truly fell swiftly sometime in the latter half of 1932 and that his family in England did not, or could not, move to help him out financially. The downward spiral thus began.

---

[1] No English will was ever drawn up to cover interests in England. He died intestate there.

## Chapter 24

*A design commissioned by Hardcastle in April 1927 for his own tomb in Girgenti. For unexplained reasons, it was never executed and, in due course, he opted for a far simpler design.*

He had already turned to his old friend Cesare De Angelis as early as the summer of 1931 for a loan of 50,000 Lire to tide him over, to cover his immediate needs and commitments (and simultaneously his London bank – presumably still tottering on – advanced him 2,500 pounds). As it became increasingly evident that he would *not* be able to repay his debt to the hotelier, he was cornered with only one option. He would have to claw back the promised gift to Italy and instead <u>sell</u> his home to them. Given the scale of the villa, the improvements he had made to it and the dimensions of the grounds, everyone reckoned that it was easily worth over 200,000 Lire. However, when an appraisal was carried out, an additional shock lay in store: the State – unsurprisingly – set its value at a risible 75,000. The low value, they explained by way of justification, was because Alexander requested that he be allowed to live there until his death, thus delaying occupancy of the place. Alexander saw a 'down payment' of 25,000 Lire. Stalling and dithering over bureaucratic details were to delay completion of the sale until well after his death. From Viterbo in September 1932 he wrote a plaintive note to Sinatra in Agrigento ending with these words, 'please forgive these brief words, but I am <u>sick</u> because of this <u>terrible</u> crisis.' Adding to that blow, somewhere in that period, his bank failed. It was the final coup de grâce.

And then, starting December 21, 1932, the letters to Palermo began. They were nothing like the humdrum ones Alexander himself sent scarcely a month earlier to the British Consulate, such as the one that had gone off with a cheque for £10 for the annual Poppy Appeal or the other, six days later, to inform the Consulate that his subscription to The Times was now reaching him regularly. Four days before Christmas, it was a deeply shaken Henry Robert who sat down at his desk in Agrigento to write to the British diplomatic authorities. Tense months had gone by in a frantic attempt to straighten out his older brother's financial affairs. There were lucid moments, but now matters were *really* spinning out of control.

Harry H. Clark was then serving as acting-consul at Palermo, following the transfer of Major James H.H. Dodds. Clark had been the last manager of Ingham Whitaker & Company, the wine estate at Marsala and thus was a familiar face on the island, a 'useful merchant', who was the natural choice to fill Dodds's shoes.

The words from Alick's brother were painful even to pen: it was to the consular office that he was writing to 'register' his brother's disturbing mental state. Matters must have deteriorated rapidly: scarcely six days later he wrote the consulate again, begging for advice. Twenty-four hours later, a third letter went off to Palermo, then a fourth, detailing what was going on at the Villa. Servants cowered in their quarters on the compound, unable to turn back the clock, witnessing with embarrassed and furtive glances all of the unfolding drama. Alexander was shouting senselessly, followed by tears and confessionals. He had stopped eating. The babble continued. Letters went off with scratched out words, blobs of ink besmirching the stationery. His engineer-like precision and clear thinking had abandoned him. He had ceased sleeping at night and paced aimlessly across the darkened tiled floors, stumbling into furniture as he went about. The backs of his rubble-roughened hands broke out in angry red rashes and as all know, the skin is frequently an accurate barometer of the level of one's personal stress and turmoil. Here was a clear-cut example of it! If Harry for long years had been 'hapless', he was now 'helpless', simply watching on the sidelines in horror as his older sibling was revisited for the third and last time by the illness that had robbed him of a happier youth.

On April 6, 1933, the situation at home was no longer tenable and Alick was taken up the twisty hill into town, a limp and hollow shell of his former self, to the compound grounds at the very end of Viale della Vittoria. After six years building, the Provincial Psychiatric Hospital complex there had formally opened in 1931. The buildings dotted around the property were bright, fresh and new and ready to accommodate up to 600 patients. Before long, the grounds began to be soothingly landscaped with palm trees, oleanders and cacti. From one of the stone terraces, there were views out to sea: to the right, just below, stood the Temple of Herakles and, to the left, of Concordia. In between, the Villa Aurea could be glimpsed. It was less than a mile away, as the crow flew. But like a desert mirage, his home was now unreachable. He could reach out his hand to try to grasp it, so seemingly near, yet never manage to touch it. Alexander would never set foot again in the Villa Aurea, his own beloved retreat for nearly a decade and a half.

Admittance into the civic hospital had originally been considered, then rejected. Set in from the Via Atenea, it was old and decrepit, damp and forbidding, hemmed in on all sides by tall, brooding buildings. Privacy there was not an option. It was no place to inflict on the disturbed English gentleman; simply out of the question. Even at the new psychiatric hospital, his Agrigento friends like Sinatra and De Angelis were mindful of the niceties: their sick friend's station in life had to be respected. Alexander would *not* be placed amidst the other patients. Instead, protectively, they arranged accommodation in the admissions building, a graceful four-story villa, just beyond the front gate, well out of earshot from the agitated outbursts of other patients. It was roomy and not yet fully occupied. Elegant wooden shutters muted the piercing sunlight and high ceilings kept the rooms cool.

Crossing through the entrance hall, Alexander looked high above him. Two Corinthian columns stood there in the atrium and between them on the stuccoed cross beam was etched an eerie quote, its wording worthy of Luigi Pirandello. Its enigmatic words about the insane read:

**QUI NON TUTTI CI SONO
E NON TUTTI LO SONO**[2]

Sadly, Alexander *was* there and he *was* insane, at least by the criteria of those times. Equally sadly, the therapeutic tools to hand in the Agrigento of 1933 were few, and by today's yardsticks, dubious. Doctors of today might well have reworded the diagnosis and termed his condition post-traumatic stress disorder, given his experiences during the Boer War. And unquestionably, they would have gone about helping him in an entirely different manner. There to meet him in his new quarters was a resident psychiatrist and the hospital's vice-director, Arturo Vitello. Vitello would be his caretaker in the coming months and duly register Hardcastle's state throughout on the clinical records. These files note that he was 'visibly pale', that his muscle tone was weak and, far worse, that he had 'suicidal tendencies'.

Between the middle of the 1800s and the early 1900s, bizarre and desperate 'cures' and therapies were in vogue. Radical treatments were being adopted, momentarily remaining in place, then jettisoned. Such gimcrackery as 'electrotherapy' had been experimented and dismissed already, as were laxative cures ('Diarrhoea very often proves a natural cure of insanity', stated one 19th-century London doctor). Hydrotherapy was tried on yet others; patients were being pummelled with high-pressure jets of water, which purportedly had a calming effect on the agitated. At the Agrigento Psychiatric

---

[2]Trans: Not all are here And not all here are.

Hospital the year of Hardcastle's admission, two courses of action were then in use: electro-convulsive therapy and pyrogenics. The latter route – by then in use in Italy since the early 1920s - was chosen for Alexander and it consisted in fever inducement. Raising a patient's temperature artificially in order to treat the mentally ill was the brainchild of a gruff-looking Vienna psychiatrist, Julius Wagner-Jauregg. Following early work dating back to the 1880s, when he initially investigated the effects of febrile diseases on psychosis, Wagner-Jauregg later resumed his experiments with a shell shocked soldier suffering contemporaneously from malaria. Blood was drawn from the young military man and injected into three other patients with motor paralysis at the Vienna clinic. Before long, they, like the soldier, were registering high fevers and after a time, showed encouraging signs of mental improvement. Soon, the Austrian doctor's fever cure was tried on every condition imaginable within psychiatry, including schizophrenia. The Austrian doctor went on to earn a Nobel Prize in physiology for his work in this field in 1927. Fever inducement was to be tried on Hardcastle right away that early spring day of 1933. Injected daily with an increasing dosage of Sulfidrol, well into early May, the hoped for high fever came slowly but brought no perceivable improvements to his morale.

*The Insane Asylum, Girgenti.*

Alexander languished for another month, his anguished thoughts never abandoning him. He was a failure, he kept repeating to the doctors, and it went back, as always, to his war experience in South Africa. He scribbled a crazed letter recording his 'sins', including that of simulating sickness in order to be shipped home. For that, he said, he should have been tortured and put into prison. He ranted that he 'showed the white feather', an expression lost on the baffled hospital staff. It was a phrase to describe having been engaged 'in acts of extreme cowardice', particularly in battle. He could not be persuaded that his breakdown was genuine. Otherwise, people told him, he would not have been evacuated. And nor would he have been awarded that medal, had his conduct been cowardly. Paradoxically, while his financial calamities had been the catalyst that triggered the final mental breakdown, it was once again the dust-covered ghosts of a war 32 years earlier that crowded in on his confused thoughts.

Things remained stationary, with no reversal in his condition. The nearby thuds and the dust of the new railroad station rising at the start of Viale della Vittoria[3] no longer disturbed him. As he grew weaker and weaker, not even injections of pick-me-up tonics, which began on June 10$^{th}$, appeared to help. At noon of June 27, as faint, tinny bells from a distant church pealed out the hour and the Sicilian sun beat down at its fiercest, his heart gave out and Alexander Hardcastle, aged 60, slipped away from life in his hospital bed there in Agrigento.[4]

When his trusted friend of nearly thirteen years, Francesco Sinatra, whose life had become so entwined with his own, sensed the end nearing, he sat down to draft the moving nine-page oration which he would deliver days later from his doorstep on the Viale della Vittoria, so near to the insane asylum.

To the townfolk gathered around him, Sinatra recalled all the vital archaeological work his friend had accomplished. He paid tribute to the deceased Englishman's civic achievements, remembering the extension of the water pipes into the Valley, the troughs for thirsty animals, the fountains, the public tree plantings. 'Today, as we devotedly follow his cortège, we pay great homage to this man who lived *in* Agrigento and *for* Agrigento. [He was] a pilgrim to our land [and] he loved it as greatly as any of its own most dedicated sons.' With that, the silent procession of mourners made its way slowly down the hill, led by Harry, the podestà, the president of the province. Removing their hats in respect as the coffin passed by, humble day labourers and farmers fell in with the train as it entered the gates of Bonamarone and made its way past tombs and marble mausolea to the very far end. Amidst the cypress trees that Alexander himself had planted, his coffin was quietly lowered into the ground and the stone he also had had carved and had left waiting was gently set over his final resting place. It read :

**ETERNITATI**
**Capitano Alexander Hardcastle**
**Commendatore della Corona d'Italia**
**Nato Londra 25.10.1872**
**Morto 27. 6.1933**

---

[3] The station was inaugurated four months after his death.
[4] Curiously, there are documentary discrepancies over his death-date. Both the entry on his Agrigento hospital records and the certificate filed with the Register of Deaths in London (with information supplied by his brother Henry) give June 26. The date on his gravestone appears as June 27.

If Sinatra's effusive words of farewell on the doorstep of his Viale della Vittoria home leaned on the florid, perhaps Hardcastle himself would have favoured as an epitaph the spartan, bare-boned words onced uttered by Pirro Marconi: '… a foreigner by birth, an Agrigentine by choice. Mæcenas of archaeology and of many works useful to mankind.' The cypresses swayed gently in the breeze. The little portal with its magnificent panoramic view out onto the Greek remains stood at the head of his tomb. Alexander was finally at rest.

# EPILOGUE

Beneath his own name and dates, Alexander's tombstone also bore details about his brother Harry: *his* name and birth date. The space remained blank where his year of death should have been because the assumption was that when the time came, he would be buried alongside Alick. A rapid rethink, however, occurred after June 27$^{th}$: now the Villa Aurea would no longer belong to a Hardcastle. His 'nurse-housekeeper' role had ended. Sicily thus fast faded as an option and he retreated, scarcely a few days after the funeral to the Villa Palanzana outside Viterbo. At least *that* place was partly his. He took his personal chattels with him, but mysteriously, most of the furnishings of Agrigento not sold off later by the Ministry of Education simply vanished without trace. Mira Francisca who was, of course, a partner in the Viterbo property rushed south to join him there and help organise an orderly retreat from Italy of her forlorn brother, taking him back to England.

Joseph Alfred had died well before the two brothers' departure for Sicily. The next Hardcastle death following Joseph Alfred's and Alick's was that of John. After his retirement in 1906 from the Royal Artillery, John remained interested in military matters for the rest of his life. He became a world authority on the scientific side of rifle shooting, introduced the pointed bullet to his country's arsenal and wrote extensively about small arms for military text books. His first two wives predeceased him and the third, Agnes Mary, outlived him. He had no children by any of them. Very much in the Herschel tradition, the tall and solidly-built John was something of a polymath. He converted to Catholicism, became an expert on the game of billiards and took up water-divining in his spare time. Family records hinted that alcoholism was a contributing factor to his death at Sidcup in April 1937.

Frances went next, eight years following Alick. After the USA and cushioned by her father's settlement on her, she continued her mathematical research and studies at Cambridge for some time and then joined the National Union of Women's Suffrage Societies in London. Following ill health and an accident, she moved north to Newcastle and built a lovely house, 'Low Bridges' at Stocksfield, 15 miles to the west, there in Northumberland countryside. It had a double arched entranceway, stone paving all around the perimeter, two chimneys and mullioned windows. During a visit to Cambridge in December 1941, she died suddenly and was buried in the Girton churchyard. Her gravestone there sets out all of her academic history and the final words read:

## Passionate Patron

*She sought knowledge:
she found Faith*

The lovely Beatrice remained a restless soul for much of her adult life, moving no fewer than eleven times around London and Cambridge. She, too, never married. She drifted from a love of drawing to the study of comparative religions. At 31, she began writing erudite pieces on esoteric eastern faiths for the monthly Theosophical Review. In little over a decade, 35 of her articles appeared in print. For twenty years, she made Crowthorne in Berkshire her home, near to where her older brother Joseph Alfred had settled his family in 1903. Yet she never visited her widowed mother at Oxted, scarcely 36 miles away. During these reclusive years she – like her brother John – succumbed to drink. She died aged 77 at The Waterloo Hotel there at Crowthorne and was buried at Wivelsfield in East Sussex in 1944.

Henry Robert never entirely shook off his reputation for indolence, even back in the bracing chill of the north. He was only 59 when he returned, yet showed no propensity to seek work, preferring instead to make do with the steady trickle of income from his father's estate. Theresa was categorical: '… from 1915 [onwards he did] nothing at all'. Félicité chimed in with a few carefully chosen words of her own: '[he was known as] Rev. Unstable – v "High" – never did *any* work! …. He became very odd, moved about during the war.' Harry enjoyed writing and did it well and amusingly when it suited him, becoming something of an epistolary gadfly in his later years. He joined The Pedestrians Association, to which Sir Max Beerbohm lent his glittering literary name as a vice-president. In his considerable free time, Harry whiled away the hours writing letters to publications railing away at such things as dirty vehicle number plates ('many drivers are tempted to leave their number-plates dirty or even to make it dirty. The law takes these insults lying down') and sparring with parliamentarians for misreporting statistics on road accidents. He wrote sermons raging against 'the ethics of smoking at the wheel' and other such topics of pale interest to others. He appears to have taken lodgings at guest houses in the south: his surviving letters come from the South View and Haskell's in Lyndhurst, where Theresa and Félicité lived, drifting later further south to Christchurch where he died aged 82, in 1956. He is interred at the crematorium in Bournemouth.

Although she was remembered as 'a great character', little information survives about Mira Francisca's adulthood. Never quite the beauty as Beatrice and Eleanor, Mira corralled her dark frizzy hair into a bun, donned owlish glasses and got on with humanitarian and scholarly pursuits, never marrying. She worked for five years
in the Bermondsey Medical Mission in London's Grange Road, founded by Selena Fox in 1904. The Mission ran an infirmary dispensing medical help as well as a soup kitchen to feed indigent women and children. Perhaps it was because of the medical milieu experienced there that she later headed for France in the aftermath of The Great War, based at Charny-sur-Meuse where she spent four years. Somewhere in her middle years, she also served as a 'sanitary inspector' and earned a first degree in dentistry. She was admitted as a Fellow to the Royal Astronomical Society in London in early 1932 and

wrote charming reminiscences of her paternal grandfather and of her uncle for the Society's monthly journal, The Observatory in the mid-1930s. Very much the guardian of family history, she often wrote to the newspapers if they erred on a detail concerning her ancestors. One amusing photograph of her from the family albums shows her dressed up in an evocation of her great grandfather William Herschel, in breeches, dress coat, propped on a cane, trying to keep a serious mien for the camera. For a long time, her home was at Stephen's Orchard, Grayshott, near Hindhead in Surrey. It was a 2-story brick house surrounded by woods. At the end, though, she moved into the Moorhill House Hotel at Burley. She died in a Hampshire nursing home aged 86, in March 1957.

*June 1934, Mira Francisca at the Runnymede Pageant imperstonating her great-grandfather Sir William Herschel as he was in June 1816. That year, he was knighted by the Prince Regent (later George IV); presumably the medal she wears is that of the Royal Guelfic Order, handed down from her ancestor. (Courtesy of D.H. Perceval)*

Eleanor Constance, 'Kiddy', was the final sibling of Alexander's to go. Her mother was enormously proud of her musical tastes and her tall, thin beauty. As she matured, Kiddy became 'spiritually minded' and, as her sister-in-law wrote, 'did much work in the Knighthood started by Miss Hankey.'[1] She later settled with a lady companion, a Miss Petty, at a gardened property called 'Little Holt' in Farnham, then moved to another Farnham address where she died in 1969, aged 89.

Today there are only two descendents from Alexander's immediate family: the granddaughters Gabrielle and Debonnaire, of his brother Joseph Alfred. The former lives in Canada and the latter in Ireland.

Pirro Marconi left Sicily in 1931 to join the Superintendency at Ancona, but kept in touch with Hardcastle. From there, he moved briefly on to teaching jobs at the universities of Cagliari and Naples. In 1936, he was appointed to lead the Italian archaeological mission in Albania and pursued notable excavations there, at Butrint. He died in an air crash over Formia in April 1938.

Francesco Sinatra lived on another 28 years after Alexander's death, ever involved in the cultural welfare of his city. Much in the same generous spirit of his English friend, Sinatra, together with his brother Giuseppe, bequeathed the latter's prized art collection to Agrigento. Paolo Orsi remained in Syracuse up until 1934, when he left. He died in 1935.

The Hotel Belvedere remains at the same Via San Vito address in the centre of Agrigento, owned and managed by Cesare De Angelis's son, Gabriele.

Beginning in 1934, the Hardcastle survivors started the labyrinthine process to hand the Villa Aurea in Agrigento over to Italy. It took three years to clear all the hurdles between notarising signatures, authentications, translations, drafting the pertinent documents and sending them to and fro, between Italy and England. In a room of the Ministry of Education on July 16, 1937, the Villa Aurea finally and formally changed ownership. Of the original price of 75,000 Lire, Alexander had seen that down payment of 25,000 Lire. The balance went directly to reimburse the loan from Cesare De Angelis. The Hardcastle siblings came away empty-handed but free from any and all future entanglements. Since Alexander's death, the Villa Aurea has undergone significant transformation. While the terrace remains largely untouched with the tiled paving, raised flower beds and stone benching still intact, the interior has been totally gutted and reshaped, to accommodate lecture and exhibition space. Over the years, it has undergone name and management changes. At present it is headquarters of the Archaeological and

---

[1] There were two non-related Miss Hankeys of evangelical note in the mid-1800s. The older was Arabella C. Hankey (1834-1911) who was best-known for writing a 50-stanza poem 'The Old, Old Story', turned into a loved church hymn. It was, however, Beatrice Hankey (1858-1933) to whom Theresa was referring. One of ten children of George Hankey, Beatrice was born at Barnet. In her thirties, with a legacy from her father, she built a mission hall on the Kentish coast where she conducted Bible classes for 700-800 attendees. She adopted the name 'Help' and went on to organise a fellowship of like-minded evangelicals. It was called 'The Knighthood'. The movement ran Bible lessons, advocated both abstinence and temperance and helped the needy, largely in the colliery towns of Wales.

Landscape Park of the Valley of the Temples and styles itself as a 'Multimedia Antiquarium', under the overall aegis of the Regional Heritage *Assessorato*. A bronze bust of Hardcastle stands in the front courtyard of the villa compound.

*Bronze bust of Alexander Hardcastle in the courtyard of the Villa Aurea. (Photo: the author)*

Outside Viterbo, the Villa Palanzana remained in Mira Francisca and Henry Robert's hands until 1938. By then, with war a possibility and with a fascist government increasingly ill-disposed towards foreigners, visits to Italy were more difficult for the two. Back in Anselmi's office, they formally renounced all holds over the house and the property fully reverted to the Balestra family. Today it houses the church-run San Crispino centre for the rehabilitation of drug addicts, the Centro Italiano di Solidarietà San Crispino. Very few changes have taken place to the villa: Alexander's name and coat-of-arms still remain over the front door. At the Theatre at Ferento, meanwhile, the marble tablet bearing Alexander's name still stands high on a wall in the entranceway. As he always envisaged, it is very much alive today giving open-air summer performances.

But it was in Agrigento that Alexander Hardcastle left his greatest mark. The *piazzale* by the entranceway into the Valley of the Temples today bears his name, as does another Agrigento street. A small group of academics and writers, headed by a local writer, Ermogene La Foreste, have started the Alexander Hardcastle Foundation to perpetuate the Englishman's memory and to mark the anniversary of his death at the cemetery each year.

The quintessential Italophile, Hardcastle came to Agrigento under trying conditions and <u>stayed</u>. He was not a professional archaeologist and nor an 'in-and-then-out-again' dabbler at the beck and call of another deep-pocketed patron. There was no country cottage back in England to which he planned to retire. Agrigento *was* home! Like Evans in Crete, he reached into his own pockets to carry out his mission. Exclusively, he saw Agrigento as his steady, lifetime *oeuvre*, to be carried out as self-effacingly as possible. Very much a man of the Victorian era, he believed in Good Works as well and led the way towards bettering his adopted city and spending a great deal of money towards that end. In all, it is reckoned that he disbursed at least one million Lire of those times on Agrigento alone.

He had a sense of vision at a time when most around him did not: tourism, he presciently reckoned, would bring the kiss of life that Agrigento so desperately needed. To attract the sort of numbers of visitors he hoped for meant bringing the ancient Greek monuments back to their fullest glory and uncovering yet more treasures from the earth. In large measure, he succeeded in that mission.

The city of Agrigento continues to grow, now counting a population of 59,000. The Valley has been placed on the United Nations World Heritage List; archaeological excavations and conservation work carry on. The town continues to do battle with unchecked illegal construction in the area. As Alexander wished, the temples today lend themselves as dramatic backdrop to theatrical performances, exhibitions, the spring almond blossom festival and a host of other cultural events. Disgorged by an army of busses, over 650,000 visitors stream through the gates each year.

The townspeople there have an even more enduring spectacle before them every single night of their lives: as the sun goes down over Agrigento and the breathtaking lights are switched on, illuminating column after column built by their very own ancestors millennia ago, it is hoped that a thought is spared for the ascetic Englishman who once was in their midst.

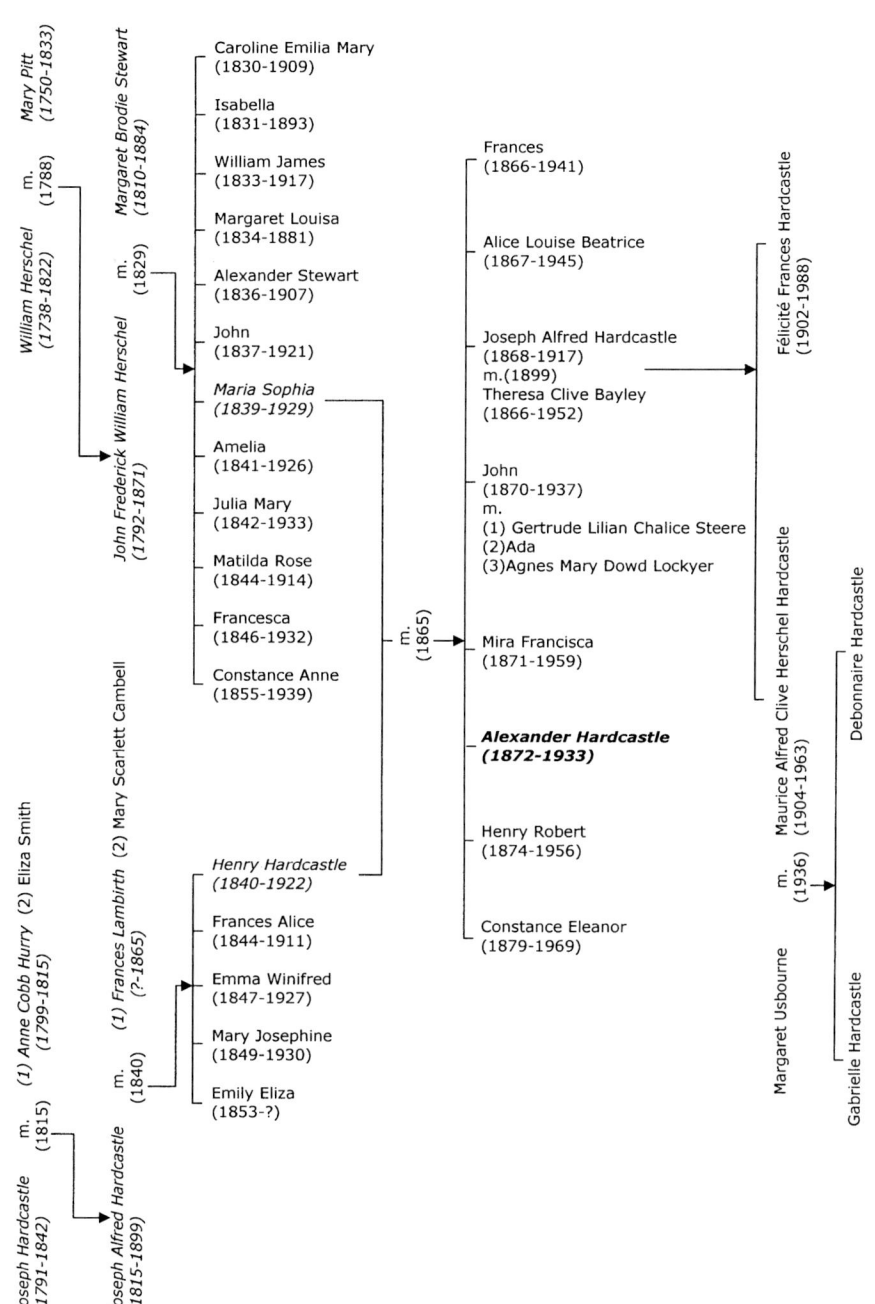

*Hardcastle Family Tree.*

# SOURCES

**Primary Sources:**

Personal archives of Debonnaire Hardcastle Perceval, Ireland. Hardcastle and Herschel family papers, albums, correspondence.

Personal archives of John Herschel Shorland, England. Hardcastle and Herschel correspondence.

Personal archives of Prof. Clemente Marconi, Italy. Correspondence of Alexander Hardcastle to Pirro Marconi.

Archives of the Soprintendenza all'Archeologia per l'Etruria Meridionale, Rome, Italy. Official correspondence concerning Hardcastle in Viterbo area.

Archives of the Soprintendenza Beni Culturali ed. Ambientali, Agrigento, Italy. Official correspondence concerning Hardcastle in Agrigento.

Archives of the Maria Mitchell Association in Nantucket, Massachusetts and of Vassar College, in Poughkeepsie, New York. The papers of Maria Mitchell.

Archives of the Theosophical Society, London.

Archives of the Harrow School, England. The academic records and photographs of Alexander and Joseph Alfred Hardcastle and the correspondence of Gerald Du Maurier.

Archivio Notarile Distrettuale di Viterbo, Viterbo.

Probate Office, London. The wills of Maria Sophia, Alexander and other Hardcastle family members.

Harry Ransom Humanities Research Center, University of Texas at Austin. John F. Herschel letters to his family and friends from Sicily.

The Royal Engineers Museum and Library, Chatham. Original transcripts regarding the Ninth Field Company, R.E., during the Boer War.

Public Records Office of Northern Ireland, Belfast. 'The Templehouse Papers at Ballymote, County Sligo.'

Public Records Office, Kew. British Consular Reports from Palermo 1921-1933.

**Books:**

**AGRIGENTO Authors** (various): *Agrigentini Illustri 1890-1940, Vols. I, II,* Agrigento, 2001.

**ARIAS, PAOLO E.**: *Quattro Archeologi del Nostro Secolo,* Pisa, 1976.

**BAGET, DOSIA**: *Shadows of the War,* London, 1901.

**BARBANERA, MARCELLO**: *L'archeologia degli italiani,* Rome, 1998.

**BASTIN, JOHN** (Compiled and Introduced by): *Travellers' Singapore,* Kuala Lumpur, 1994.

**BELL, LELAND, V.**: *Treating the Mentally Ill from Colonial Times to the Present,* New York, 1980.

**BOWEN, EDWARD**: *A Memoir,* London, 1902.

**BOYD, DEREK**: *The Royal Engineers,* London, 1975.

**BROWN, ASHLEY**: *Sicily Present and Past,* London 1928.

**BUTTMANN, GUNTHER**: *The Shadow of the Telescope,* London, 1974.

**CAMERON, JULIA M.**: *The Cameron Collection. An Album of Photographs,* Wokingham, 1975.

**DATO, GIUSEPPE**: *Le Vie dello Zolfo in Sicilia,* Rome, 1991.

**DENNIS, GEORGE**: *The Cities and Cemeteries of Etruria,* London, 1878.
   - *A Handbook for Travellers in Sicily,* London, 1864.

**DU MAURIER, DAPHNE**: *Gerald: A Portrait,* London, 1934.

**ELLIOTT, FRANCES:** *The Diary of an Idle Woman in Sicily,* London, 1881.

**EMERSON, ISABEL:** *Things Seen in Sicily,* London, 1929.

**FIORENTINI, GRAZIELLA** (A cura di): *Introduzione alla Valle dei Templi,* Agrigento. N.d.

**GERNSHEIM, HELMUT:** *Famous Photographers,* London, 1848.

**GIRLING, BRIAN** (Compiled by): *Westminster's Villages,* Stroud, 1996.

**GIUDICE, GASPARE:** *Pirandello – A Biography,* London, 1975.

**GOLDING, LOUIS:** *Sicilian Noon,* New York, 1926.

**GUGGISBERG, Captain F.G.:** *The Shop Story 1900-1939,* Woolwich, 1954.

**HARDCASTLE, HENRY:** *The Law and Practice of Election Petitions,* London, 1874.

**HARDING, JAMES:** *Gerald Du Maurier: The Last Actor-Manager*, London 1989.

**HOARE, PHILIP:** *Spike Island: The Memory of a Military Hospital,* London 2001.

**HOBHOUSE, HERMIONE:** *Thomas Cubitt: Master Builder,* London, 1971.

**HODGES, RICHARD:** *Visions of Rome: Thomas Ashby, archaeologist,* Rome, 2001.

**HOLLOWAY, R. ROSS:** *The Archaeology of Ancient Sicily,* London, 2000.

**HOWSON, E.W. (and Townsend Warner, G.)** (Ed.): *Harrow School,* London, 1898.

**HUDSON, ROBERT:** *A Life of King George V,* London, 1930.

**HUTTON, EDWARD:** *Cities of Sicily,* London, 1926.

**JACKSON, MRS NEVILLE:** *A Student in Sicily,* London, 1926.

**JONES, HENRY FESTING:** *Diversions in Sicily,* London, 1909.

**LABORDE, E.D.:** *Harrow School Yesterday and Today,* London, 1948.

**LORIMER, NORMA:** *By the Waters of Sicily,* London, 1901.

**LUBBOCK, CONSTANCE A.** (Edit.): *The Herschel Chronicle,* London, 1933.

**MACK SMITH, D. and FINLAY, M.I., DUGGAN, C.:** *A History of Sicily,* London 1986.

**MARCONI, PIRRO:** *Agrigento Arcaica,* Rome, 1933.
- *Agrigento: Topografia ed Arte,* Florence, 1929.

**MASTERS, ROY:** *The Royal Arsenal, Woolwich,* Stroud, 1995.

**MAURICE-JONES, COL. K.W.:** *The Shop Story 1900-1939,* Woolwich, 1954.

**MERTONS, DIETER:** *Città e monumenti dei greci d'occidente,* Rome, 2006.

**MICCICHE, GIUSEPPE:** *Dopoguerra e Fascismo in Sicilia,* Rome, 1976.

**MILLER, HELEN HILL:** *Sicily and the Western Colonies of Greece,* New York, 1965.

**MITCHELL, PHEBE KENDALL:** *Maria Mitchell – Life, Letters and Journals,* New York 1971.

**MONKSWELL LADY (Née Mary Josephine Hardcastle):** *A Victorian Diarist 1895-1909,* London, 1946.

**MOORE, PATRICK:** *William Herschel Astronomer and Musician,* Bath, 2000.
- *Sir John Herschel Explorer of the Southern Sky,* Bath, 1992.

**NICOLOSI, PIETRO:** *50 Anni di cronaca siciliana 1900-1950,* Palermo, 1975.

**PAGET, LADY WALBURGA:** *Embassies of Other Days,* London, 1923.

**PALILLO, ANGELO:** *Agrigento Turistica,* Agrigento, 1996.

**PEMBLE, JOHN:** *The Mediterranean Passion Victorians and Edwardians in the South,* Oxford, 1987.

**PENSABENE, PATRIZIO:** *Il Teatro di Ferento,* Rome, 1989.

*Sources*

**PICONE, GIUSEPPE:** *Memorie Storiche Agrigentine, Vol. I,* Agrigento, 1934.

**PIRANDELLO, LUIGI:** *Novelle per un Anno, Volume 9,* Florence, 1925.

**POWELL, ANNE (Edit.):** *Felicité Hardcastle A Unique New Forest Lady,* Burley, 1989.

**RANDALL-MACIVER, DAVID:** *Greek Cities in Italy and Sicily,* Oxford, 1931.

**RANDALL-MACIVER, JOANNA:** *Letters from Abroad,* (privately printed), Oxford, 1934.

**READ, C.S.:** *Military Psychiatry in Peace and War,* London, 1920.

**RESTIFO, GIUSEPPE:** *Tourism and the History of Taormina, Sicily 1750-1950,* Lewiston, 2000.

**RHODES, D.E.:** *Dennis of Etruria: the Life of George Dennis,* London, 1973.

**RIGGIO, GAETANO:** *Vita e cultura agrigentina del '900,* Caltanissetta, 1978.

**RIVELA, A, and PERNULL, H.V.:** *The Dead Cities of Sicily,* Palermo, 1905.

**ROGERS, H.C.B.:** *Troopships and their history,* London, 1963.

**SLADEN, DOUGLAS:** *Sicily the New Winter Resort,* London, 1903.

**TREVELYAN, RALEIGH:** *Princes under the Volcano,* London, 2002.

**TURNBULL, C.M.:** *A History of Singapore 1819-1975,* London, 1980.

**TWEEDIE, MRS ALEX (Ethel Brilliana):** *Sunny Sicily,* London, 1904.

**TYERMAN, CHRISTOPHER:** *A History of Harrow School 1324-1991,* Oxford, 2000.

**VALENSTEIN, ELLIOT:** *Great and Desperate Cures,* New York, 1986.

**WATSON, COL.SIR CHARLES:** *The History of the Corps of the Royal Engineers,* Vol. 3, Chatham, 1915.

**WOOLEY, LEONARD:** *Dead Towns and Living Men,* London, 1920.
- *As I Seem to Remember It,* London, 1962.

**WRIGHT, HELEN:** *Sweeper in the Sky The Life of Maria Mitchell,* New York, 1950.


**Other material:**

'Alexander Hardcastle: l'uomo, l'archeologo, il suo tempo.' Edited by Pio Luigi Lo Bue, Atti del 1° Convegno su A. Hardcastle - 27 June 1984.

'Un Mecenate Inglese fra i Templi di Agrigento - Sir Alexander Hardcastle', Isabella Scichilone (University Thesis) 1997.

Alumni Cantabrigiensis, Part 2, Vol. 3, Cambridge, 1942, p.232.

American Journal of Archaeology, Vol. 33, 1929, pp. 440-443.

Anglo-Italian Review, Vol. 2, n. 3, 'The Sicilian Sulphur Industry', March 1921.

Antiquity, various issues.

Baedeker's Guide to Southern Italy, London, 1908.

Boyles' Court and County Guides, London, various years.

The Century Illustrated Magazine, Vol. 3, 1889, pp. 903-909.

Chapman, Allan: 'An Occupation for an Independent Gentleman: Astronomy in the Life of John Herschel.' Abstract adapted from Vistas in Astronomy, Vol. 36, No.1, Wadham College, Oxford, 1993, pp. 71-116.

Connolly, T.W.J., Roll of Officers of the Corps of Royal Engineers from 1660-1898, Chatham, 1898.

Corriere della Sera, March 18, 1925.

Crockford's Clerical Directory, London, 1933.

Essex County Chronicle (Chelmsford), September 26, 1901.

Ferento Guida agli Scavi, Augusto Gargana, Viterbo, 1935.

The Girton Review, Cambridge, Easter term, 1942.

The Haileyburian, June 3, 1937.

Harrow School Register 1885-1949, edited by James A. Moir, London, 1951.

Illustrated London News, various issues.

Journal of Hellenic Studies, Vol. 56, 1936, p. 239.

Journal of the Royal Engineers (supplement), September 1933, p. 245.

Marconi, Pirro Commemoration speech by Prof. Biagio Pace, Naples, 1939.

Morning Post, July 22, 1922.

The New York Times, various issues.

Notizie degli Scavi di Antichità, Reale Accademia Nazionale dei Lincei, Rome, Various volumes.

Novissima Guida Storico-artistico di Girgenti e dei suoi monumenti, A. Cremona, Girgenti, 1925.

Nuove Ipotesi, 'Ricordo di Pirro Marconi', by Elio Di Bella, N. 4, July-August 1988.

Oxford Dictionary of National Biography, Oxford, 2004, various entries.

The Pedestrian Association's Quarterly News Letter – N. 8 (April 1934) and N. 48 (February 1945)

'Resurrezione del tempio di Ercole a Girgenti', by Luigi Biagi in Le Vie d'Italia, TCI, 1924.

Ridgway, David: 'David Randall-MacIver (1873-1945)', Vol. 69 (1983) From the proceedings of The British Academy, London.

'Rivista' (British-Italian Society), N. 389 Summer 2006.

Royal Engineers Journal, December 1, 1900, pp. 247-249.

Slough, Eton and Windsor Observer, April 10, 1936.

Surrey Mirror & County Post, November 16, 1917.

Time Magazine, March 2, 1925.

The Times, various issues.

Who Was Who 1929-1940, London.

Zanotti-Bianco, U.: 'Paolo Orsi', A Cura dell'Archivio Storico per la Calabria e la Lucania, Rome, 1935.

# ABOUT THE AUTHOR

Alexandra Richardson was born in New York and has lived much of her adult life in Italy. She has worked in Bangkok for USIA, New York for Newsweek Magazine and Milan for Selezione dal Reader's Digest. With her husband, she lives between London and Tuscany.